T0089150

Spelling Matters

R. Kent Smith & Shawn J. Smith

ARCHWAY PUBLISHING

Archway Publishing books may be ordered through booksellers or by contacting:

Archway Publishing
1663 Liberty Drive
Bloomington, IN 47403
www.archwaypublishing.com
844-669-3957

ISBN: 978-1-4808-9300-9 (sc)
ISBN: 978-1-4808-9301-6 (e)

Library of Congress Control Number: 2020913181

Print information available on the last page.

Archway Publishing rev. date: 09/28/2020

CONTENTS

INTRODUCTION

The title of this book, **Spelling Matters,** is meant to convey two meanings:

- spelling <u>matters</u> because good spelling is essential to the understanding of written communication
- good spelling involves many <u>matters</u>, which this book addresses in a comprehensive manner

Although some people appear to be naturally good spellers of English with little apparent effort (they are generally gifted sight readers who need few exposures to words to master their spellings; they are also likely to be voracious readers), there are legitimate reasons why others often find English spelling words frequently frustrating. For example, consider these words: (1) those that sound the same but are spelled differently (pail, pale); (2) those that possess the same letter combination but have different pronunciations (t<u>h</u>ough, <u>rough</u>); (3) those that contain silent letters (<u>k</u>ne<u>e</u>, nigh<u>t</u>); those beginning with *c*, which sometimes has a *k* sound (caught, crack) but at other times has an *s* sound (center, cement) (5) those words containing an unstressed syllable with a *schwa* sound (*ah*), a sound represented by an upside down *e* (ə), but with the *schwa* sound it can be difficult to detect which vowel (*a, e, i, o, u*) is representing it; notice, for example, the pronunciation of "grammar" sounds pretty much the same whether you spell it GRAMM <u>a</u>r, GRAMM <u>e</u>r, GRAMM <u>i</u>r, GRAMM <u>o</u>r, or GRAMM <u>u</u>r (the correct spelling is *GRAMM <u>a</u>r*); (6) those words that are exceptions to traditional spelling rules, such as the following:

> <u>i</u> before <u>e</u> *(fr<u>ie</u>nd, n<u>ie</u>ce)* except after <u>c</u> *(c<u>ei</u>ling, rec<u>ei</u>pt)* or when sounded like *n<u>ei</u>ghbor or w<u>ei</u>gh.*

Unfortunately, there are numerous exceptions to this spelling rule, as ***Spelling Matters*** will point out.

But despite the spelling challenges that exist, most people can become above-average or excellent spellers. In fact, chances are that people who succeed (and you are probably one of them) in sports, music, art, carpentry, or a host of other activities, have likely overcome many more challenges than those involved in spelling, so you can be confident that you can become (if you're not already) an above-average speller of English words if you make that your goal.

This book may be profitably used by a broad range of learners—including high school, college, ESL, and adult educational students—and is adaptable to both individual/private and group/classroom use. Though it focuses largely on commonly misspelled words, it also includes challenging ones often required for more advanced writing. Whatever your circumstances, you are most likely to maximize your improvement in spelling by adhering to the following guidelines.

General Suggestions

- Work through ***Spelling Matters*** on a consistent basis (even ten to fifteen minutes three or four times a week will pay dividends), and review those chapters you need to concentrate on as indicated by your results on the spelling pre-assessment and chapter check-ups.
- Become an avid reader and writer if you aren't already, as regular reading and writing will familiarize you with many of the words whose correct spelling you will find beneficial to know.
- When you type on a computer, use the computer's spelling and grammar check to discover whether any corrections need to be made.
- Keep a list of words you find especially difficult to spell. You may find this ***Three-W Steps Method*** helpful in mastering these words:

  1. _WRITE_   *the word in large script;*
  2. _WRITE_   *the word in the air with your eyes shut;*
  3. _WRITE_   *the word on paper; check to make sure you have spelled the word correctly.*

Getting Started

Do the *Pre-Assessment* that follows. Your results on the *Pre-Assessment* can guide you as to which chapters might deserve your special attention. Answers to the *Pre-Assessment*, chapter exercises and check-ups, and *Post-Assessment* are included in the *Answer Key* located in the back of the book.

PRE-ASSESSMENT

Chapter 1, Noun Plurals

Write the plural form of the nouns that follow.

	singular	*plural*
1.	donkey	_____
2.	valley	_____
3.	community	_____
4.	apology	_____
5.	solo	_____
6.	half	_____
7.	mother-in-law	_____
8.	canoe	_____
9.	bus	_____
10.	church	_____

Chapter 2, *-ei*, *-ie* Words

Neatly circle the correctly spelled word.

1.	theif	thief	6.	feild	field
2.	weight	wieght	7.	vein	vien
3.	beleive	believe	8.	neighbor	nieghbor
4.	neice	niece	9.	seizure	siezure
5.	ceiling	cieling	10.	beleif	belief

Chapter 3, Vowel Suffixes

Write the correctly spelled word in the line provided.

_____ 1. Sandy went (joging, jogging) a few minutes ago.

_____ 2. It (occurred, occured) to me that our sales department could use an energetic person like you.

_____ 3. Sharon gets her exercise by (swiming, swimming) three mornings a week.

_____ 4. Why are you (quizzing, quizing) me about my whereabouts last night?

_____ 5. My mother always (prefered, preferred) tea to coffee in the morning.

_____ 6. Merton made a (courageous, couragous) attempt to overcome his health problems.

_____ 7. We've (picniced, picnicked) many times at Lake Armstrong State Park.

_____ 8. The weather is (changeable, changable) in April, isn't it?

_____ 9. Bob Feller, who pitched for the Cleveland Indians, became (fameous, famous) while still a teenager.

_____ 10. Fletcher, it's (inconceivable, inconceiveable) to many people that you've become a successful minister because you were such a holy terror when you were growing up.

Chapter 4, Prefixes, Compounds, Consonant Suffixes, Final -y Words

Neatly circle the correct answer.

1. Mrs. Donaldson, ninety-six years old, was shocked when the clerk said he'd have to do a (back ground, background) check on her before he could sell her an umbrella.

2. My college (roommate, roomate) is from Florida.

3. Many of the (Murphies, Murphys) are over six feet tall.

4. Sandra's degree is in business (management, managment).

5. Your recital was simply (gloryous, glorious), darling.

6. George often (studys, studies) at the campus coffee shop.

7. Melissa is the (bookkeeper, bookeeper) for the law firm.

8. Manuel said his (happyness, happiness) depends upon the price he can get for his oranges.

9. My remarks were (unecessary, unnecessary) because everybody already knew that Francine and Lucky were getting married this fall.

10. Our (mailbox, mail box) was stuffed with magazines.

Chapters 5 and 6, Words Frequently Confused

Neatly circle the correct word.

1. Whee! I am so relieved that I (passed, past) my genetics exam! The (affect, effect) on me is that I am now determined to become a world-renowned medical researcher and discover why many teenagers often have acne.

2. In my immediate (passed, past), I was a trail guide at a dude ranch in Utah.

3. "So Uncle John, you prefer to watch old movies on TV rather (than, then) play hop-scotch with me?" whined Debbie, his twenty-six-year-old niece.

4. What (advice, advise) would you give to a recent high school graduate about what to (wear, where) when they go for a job interview, Count Dracula?

5. Mr. and Mrs. Johnson are going to the Black Hills in June; in fact, (their, there, they're) (hole, whole) family is going (their, there, they're).

6. (Their, There, They're) hoping that it won't be (to, too, two) hot (their, there, they're) this summer.

7. (Wear, Where) is the bus station?

8. Thursday was (quit, quiet, quite) nice as the temperature climbed to fourteen degrees, and (its, it's) only the first of May.

9. The cross-country (coarse, course) is in good shape despite all the snow and rain.

10. I was embarrassed as my glasses were in (plain, plane) sight on the kitchen table.

11. The (personal, personnel) office at Money Maker's Bank on Rocky Hill Road closes at 5:00 p.m.

12. "Are you (threw, through) reading the paper?" Flossie asked.

13. Do you think that the Buttercups will (loose, lose) to the Loony Birds today?

14. "Rita, how much more (capital, capitol) do you think we will need before we can open our own shoes and bags store?" asked Billy Joe.

15. My elderly neighbor said he's in perfect health (accept, except) for his itchy scalp and twitchy nose.

16. Dale wasn't (conscience, conscious) of the fact that he had asked (to, too, two) many (personal, personnel) questions of our guest, so his (conscience, conscious) didn't bother him.

Chapters 7 and 8, Spelling Challenges 1, 2

In the line provided, write "correct" if the word is spelled correctly; if the word is misspelled, write its correct spelling.

1. incidently   _____

2. aquittal   _____

3. valuable   _____

4. tragedy   _____

5. amatuer   _____

6. miniture   _____

7. sandwich   _____

8. bachelor   _____

9. reccomend   _____

10. enviroment   _____

11. boundry   _____

12. sophmorc   _____

13. recognize   _____

14. mathamatics   _____

15. quanity   _____

16. occurance   _____

17. disapline   _____

18. comittee   _____

19. accomodate   _____

20. advisible   _____

Chapter 9, Academic Words

Neatly circle the correctly spelled word.

1. hypothesis   hypothisis

2. behavor   behavior

3. cognitive   cognative

4. catalist   catalyst

5. analyze   analize

6. benine   benign

7. malignent   malignant

8. empiracal   empirical

9. curiculem   curriculum

10. author   auther

Chapter 10, Capital Letters

In the sentences that follow, underline any word or words that SHOULD or SHOULD NOT begin with a capital letter. Then, on the line provided, correctly rewrite these words. If a sentence contains no capitalization errors, write "correct" on the line.

1. Mr. Lopez has been principal at St. Michael's
   High School for many years.   _____

2. have you read the book *Get Rich Now* by Gonna Robabank?

   _____

3. When we traveled in the West, we saw few cows but lots of Cowboys.

   _____

4. *Titanic* is still one of my favorite movies," Lucille said, "But I haven't seen it again since last week."

   _____

5. My friend Harry has a 1996 Harley Davidson motorcycle that he's always kept in mint condition.

   _____

6. Flag Day is a National Holiday in the united states of america that's celebrated on June 14th every year.

   _____

7. My Uncle and Aunt have moved back to minnesota after retiring to florida six years ago. _____

8. Have you ever read the Peanuts comic strips about snoopy reading *war and peace,* but reading it just one word a day? At that rate, I think, it will take him at least a Century to read the entire book.

   _____

9. Cousin Ernie claims he was a good student in high school, particularly in Science and Geography. He also claims he became fluent in speaking Algebra by the time he was a Sophomore.

   _____

10. Ernie and his wife Isabella just returned from a trip to canada, and they said they especially enjoyed the time they spent in quebec city. Ernie also said canada was the only foreign country they had ever been in except for New Jersey.

_____

Check your answers on the Pre-Assessment you have just completed with those in the Answer Key. This comparison should prove helpful in determining which chapters may deserve your special attention.

Noun Plurals

A <u>noun</u> is a person, place, or thing, and <u>plural</u> means more than one. The vast majority of nouns are made plural by simply adding an *-s* to them, as shown in the following examples:

Singular	*Plural*
car	car<u>s</u>
avenue	avenue<u>s</u>
computer	computer<u>s</u>
instrument	instrument<u>s</u>

EXERCISE 1.1   *Write the plural form for the following nouns.*

1. tree   _____

2. animal   _____

3. chair   _____

4. magazine   _____

5. basketball _____

Plural Compound Words

The plurals of compound nouns are formed when the main word in the compound is made plural:

Singular	*Plural*
maid of honor	maid<u>s</u> of honor
son-in-law	son<u>s</u>-in-law
passer-by	passer<u>s</u>-by
attorney-at-law	attorney<u>s</u>-at-law
drive-in	drive-in<u>s</u>

EXERCISE 1.2 *Write the plural for the following compound nouns:*

1. daughter-in-law _____

2. commander-in-chief _____

3. runner-up _____

4. drive-in _____

5. mother-in-law _____

−*es*

There are other nouns that require special attention when they are pluralized, including those ending in *-s, -ch, -sh, -z* and *-x*. Because these nouns are pronounced with more than one syllable, *-es* instead of just *-s* is added to them:

Singular	*Plural*
bus	bus<u>es</u>
church	church<u>es</u>

brush	brush<u>es</u>
buzz	buzz<u>es</u>
box	box<u>es</u>

EXERCISE 1.3 *Write the plural form for each of the following nouns:*

1. beach _____

2. glass _____

3. waltz _____

4. crash _____

5. fox _____

–y

The plural of a noun ending in *-y*, if it is preceded by a vowel (*a, e, i, o, u*), is formed simply by adding *-s*:

Singular	*Plural*
valley	valley<u>s</u>
Monday	Monday<u>s</u>

If, however, the noun ends in *-y* preceded by a consonant, then drop the *-y* and add *-ies:*

Singular	*Plural*
pony	pon<u>ies</u>
company	compan<u>ies</u>

Exception: People's names ending in *-y* are made plural by simply adding *-s* regardless of whether the *-s* is preceded by a vowel or consonant:

Singular	*Plural*
Kerry	Kerry<u>s</u>
Murray	Murray<u>s</u>
Barney	Barney<u>s</u>
Lounsberry	Lounsberry<u>s</u>

EXERCISE 1.4   *Write the plural of the following nouns:*

1.   McKay   _____

2.   army   _____

3.   Friday   _____

4.   country   _____

5.   Kennedy   _____

6.   subway   _____

-o

Forming the plural of nouns ending in *-o* can be challenging (and frustrating) as can be seen by the following guidelines:

(1) Nouns ending in *-o* preceded by a vowel (*a, e, i, o, u*) are made plural by simply adding *-s*:

Singular	*Plural*
radio	radio<u>s</u>
studio	studio<u>s</u>
boo	boo<u>s</u>
zoo	zoo<u>s</u>

(2) The plural of nouns associated with music are also made plural by simply adding -*s*:

Singular	Plural
piano	pianos
solo	solos
soprano	sopranos
piccolo	piccolos

(3) Most nouns ending in -*o* preceded by a consonant are made plural by adding -*es*:

Singular	Plural
hero	heroes
tomato	tomatoes
potato	potatoes
echo	echoes

Exceptions: Unfortunately, there are exceptions to the preceding guideline, including these nouns, as you simply add -*s* to them to make them plural:

Singular	Plural
photo	photos
auto	autos
momento	momentos
Eskimo	Eskimos
Filipino	Filipinos

And just to add to the confusion, some nouns ending in -*o* can be made plural by adding *either* -*s* or -*es* (you can't go wrong!). Among such nouns are these:

Singular	Plural		
cargo	cargos	*or*	cargoes
mosquito	mosquitos	*or*	mosquitoes

tornado	tornados	or	tornadoes
desperado	desperados	or	desperadoes
volcano	volcanos	or	volcanoes
hobo	hobos	or	hoboes

And if you really want to learn of a noun whose plural form is unlikely to be misspelled, consider the word *buffalo,* as all three of these words can be considered in the plural tense: *buffalo* or *buffalos* or *buffaloes.*

EXERCISE 1.5 *Write the plural form of the following nouns that end in -o:*

1. veto   _____

2. patio   _____

3. tornado   _____

4. solo   _____

5. radio   _____

6. embargo   _____

7. mosquito   _____

8. video   _____

9. buffalo   _____

10. potato   _____

-f and *-fe*

Nouns ending in *-f* or *-fe* are made plural by simply adding *-s* to them if the basic pronunciation doesn't change dramatically:

Singular	Plural
chief	chiefs
reef	reefs
gulf	gulfs
sheriff	sheriffs
tariff	tariffs
fife	fifes

However, when the basic pronunciation changes noticeably, then drop the *-f* and add *-ves* as seen in these examples:

Singular	Plural
half	halves
leaf	leaves
wolf	wolves
knife	knives

Admittedly, it is difficult to discern whether the plural form of a noun ending in *-f* changes its pronunciation. When you find that to be the case, use your computer's spellchecker.

As was true regarding the spelling of *buffalo*, there are also various options when spelling these nouns ending in *-f*:

Singular	Plural		
dwarf	dwarfs	*or*	dwarves
hoof	hoofs	*or*	hooves
scarf	scarfs	*or*	scarves
wharf	wharfs	*or*	wharves

EXERCISE 1.6 *Write the plural form of these nouns:*

1. loaf _____

2. chief _____

3. scarf _____

4. elf _____

5. proof _____

6. thief _____

7. life _____

8. reef _____

9. tariff _____

10. gulf _____

Irregular Nouns

You are likely familiar with the plural form of these nouns:

Singular	*Plural*
man	men
woman	women
child	children
foot	feet
mouse	mice
tooth	teeth
goose	geese
ox	oxen

And you will probably recall that the plural form of some animal nouns is the same as their singular form:

Singular	Plural
deer	deer
fish	fish
salmon	salmon
trout	trout
sheep	sheep

-is

Observe how the following nouns ending in -is are made plural:

Singular	Plural
analysis	analyses
crisis	crises
diagnosis	diagnoses
parenthesis	parentheses
oasis	oases
hypothesis	hypotheses

As you can see, the plural of nouns ending in -is is formed by simply changing the -is to -es.

EXERCISE 1.7 *Write the plural of these nouns:*

1. tooth   _____

2. mouse   _____

3. parenthesis _____

4. sheep   _____

5. crisis   _____

6. oasis   _____

7. ox   _____

8. woman   _____

9. diagnosis   _____

10. salmon   _____

After reviewing the chapter, complete the Check-Up that follows.

 CHECK-UP: Chapter 1, Noun Plurals

A   ***In the space provided, write the plural form for the following nouns:***

Singular	**Plural**

1. potato   _____

2. piano   _____

3. hero   _____

4. echo   _____

5. son-in-law _____

6. box   _____

7. woman   _____

8. thief   _____

9. sheriff   _____

10. wife   _____

11. belief   _____

12. yourself   _____

13. crisis   _____

14. fish   _____

15. sheep   _____

16. analysis   _____

17. thesis   _____

18. latch   _____

19. maid of honor _____

20. bush   _____

B *Neatly circle the correctly spelled plural nouns:*

1.   cliffes   cliffs

2.   pastries   pastrys

3.   donkeys   donkies

4.   batterys   batteries

5.   themselfs   themselves

6.	tomatos	tomatoes
7.	echoes	echos
8.	lunches	lunchs
9.	Kennedys	Kennedies
10.	valleys	vallies
11.	churches	churchs
12.	moose	mooses
13.	attorney-at-laws	attorneys-at-law
14.	mouses	mice
15.	children	childrens
16.	hawks	hawkes
17.	familys	families
18.	prescriptions	prescriptiones
19.	matchs	matches
20.	analysises	analyses

C *After reading each statement, circle either True or False.*

True   *False*   1. Most nouns are made plural by simply adding *-s* to them.

True   *False*   2. On the other hand, all nouns ending in *-o* are made plural by adding *-es* to them.

True *False* 3. To make nouns ending in *-s, -ch, -sh, -z, and -x* plural, also add *-es* to them.

True *False* 4. Nouns ending in *-y* preceded by a vowel (*a, e, i, o, u*) are made plural by dropping the *-y* and adding *-ies;* however, if the *-y* is preceded by a consonant, keep the *-y* and simply add *-s.*

True *False* 5. If you wish to make a compound (split word) plural simply add *-s* to *either* noun, as this example of daughter-in-law illustrates: **daughters-in-law** *or* **daughter-in-laws**

True *False* 6. Nouns ending in *-is* are made plural by changing the *-i* in the last syllable to *-e* and retaining the *-s* as seen in this example:

S	P
neuro<u>sis</u>	neuro<u>ses</u>

True *False* 7. The plural of the family name of **Humphrey** is **Humphries**.

True *False* 8. The spelling of the plural of society is **societies**.

True *False* 9. The plural spelling of **leaf** can be either **leaf<u>s</u>** or **lea<u>ves</u>**.

True *False* 10. The plural spelling of **luxury** can be either **luxury<u>s</u>** or **luxur<u>ies</u>**.

-*ie* and -*ei* Words

The best known guideline relating to spelling of the words in this chapter is "*i* before *e* except after *c* or when sounded like *a* as in *neighbor* and *weigh*." Many people through the years have committed this guideline to memory because they have found it helpful, but, on the other hand, others have not found it particularly helpful because of the numerous exceptions to it. After working through this chapter, you can decide for yourself whether it is worth remembering.

So let's get started. First of all, notice that the following words support the "*i* before *e* ..." guideline

achieve	field	niece	retrieve
belief	fierce	obedient	shield
believe	friend	piece	shriek
brief	grief	pierce	siege
calorie	hygiene	priest	wield
cashier	mischief	quiet	yield
chief	movie	relief	

EXERCISE 2.1 *Proofread: circle the correctly spelled words.*

Twallah Terwilliger

1. I am the wonderful (but modest) Casper Whipplesnade, and I have many (freinds, friends), but Twallah, a girl I had been dating for a long time (three weeks), once had been closest to my heart.

2. Casandra, my fifteen-year-old (neice, niece), introduced me to Twallah a month ago, and Twallah and I started dating soon after. Little did I suspect that Twallah would cause me, the incomparable Casper Whipplesnade, so much (grief, greif).

3. I had found out through my best (freind, friend), Tommy Tactless, that not only was Twallah dating me, but she was sneaking behind my back and also dating Frankie Fullerbrush, the (cheif, chief) dishwasher at the Dew Drop Inn Café. A terrible (shreik, shriek) erupted from the depths of my soul when the extent of Twallah's betrayal registered with me.

4. I immediately tore through a nearby (field, feild) because it was a shortcut to the Dew Drop Inn Café. I was desperate to find out for sure if Tommy was telling me the truth. When I finally stumbled through the café door, I spotted Twallah and Frankie talking to the (cashier, casheir). Frankie and Twallah were smiling at each other while actually holding hands! I gasped, stared, and thought I would have to seek solace from my parish (preist, priest).

5. Oh, the pain of it all! I don't (beleive, believe) I had ever suffered such (fierce, feirce) agony in all my born days. My befuddled brain simply couldn't (queit, quiet) down sufficiently to process the fact that a reasonably intelligent girl like Twallah could dump me as her (boyfreind, boyfriend) for an older man— Frankie was sixteen years old, for goodness' sake!

6. Needless to say, I told Twallah that we were through, but then instead of bursting into tears as I thought she would, an expression of heavenly (relief, releif) seemed to sweep over her face. Can you (believe, beleive) it?

7. This is it, dear hearts. From now on I, Casper Whipplesnade, am going to build a (sheild, shield) around my tender heart. I will no longer (yeild, yield) to temptation and date anyone. Once again, my goal in life will be to (acheive,

achieve) inner peace and (queit, quiet). (Though I have noticed an attractive girl … but no, absolutely not, yet …)

EXERCISE 2.2 *One of the words in each group of four words is misspelled. Circle this word, then spell it correctly in the line provided.*

1. siege   calorie   retrieve   hygeine   _____

2. obediant   piece   priest   yield   _____

3. grief   friend   feild   brief   _____

4. achieve   fierce   sheild   mischief   _____

5. weild   relief   niece   chief   _____

6. pierce   shreik   quiet   cashier   _____

7. believe   hieght   brief   belief   _____

Continuing with *i* before *e* except after *c*:

ceiling	deceit	receipt
conceit	perceive	receive
conceive		

or when sounded like *a* as in *n<u>eigh</u>bor* and *w<u>eigh</u>*:

eight	neighbor	veil
feign	reign	vein
freight	sleigh	weigh
heinous	surveillance	

EXERCISE 2.3   *If the -ie word in each sentence is correct, write "Correct" in the space provided; otherwise, indicate its correct spelling.*

1. What makes you think Matilda is full of conceit?   _____

2. I severed several viens when I had an accident using my chainsaw.   _____

3. My neck was stiff and sore after I painted the dining room cieling.   _____

4. When I was in elementary school, I would sometimes fiegn illness so I wouldn't have to go to school that day.   _____

5. Minnie hopes to receive an answer today from Disney World regarding her job application.   _____

6. My nieghbor is very considerate as his numerous parties always end by 3:30 a.m.   _____

7. The busy bee remarked, "Because I weighed way too much, I went on a diet for four months, and I'm happy to report that I lost three ounces during this time!"   _____

8. My friend, I wouldn't decieve you, but I perceive that you don't believe me.   _____

9. Why can't you conceive of me winning the lottery?   _____

10. Will Miss America's riegn last for an entire year?   _____

11. A freight train went rumbling by as we waited for the bars of the gate to rise.   _____

12. Twitchy, the police sheriff, announced that the Rinky-Dinky Saloon had been robbed, the most hienous crime in Bugsbomb in many a year.   _____

13. Monty, be sure you have the receipt with you when you return the merchandise to the store.   _____

14. Hazel said she often rode in a sleigh when she was a young girl of 72.   _____

15. Hazel also said she sometimes had to pull on the reins if Zeke, her horse, began trotting too fast, like fifteen miles per hour.   _____

16. She said it took all the strength that her wieght of 236 pounds provided her to bring Zeke's blazing speed to a more reasonable five miles an hour.   _____

17. The witness said that one of the robbers wore a gold ski mask, and the other one wore a multi-colored viel.   _____

EXCEPTIONS to the *-ie* and *-ei* saying:

The guideline "*i* before *e* except after *c* or when sounded like *a* as in *neighbor* and *weigh*" can be helpful in the spelling of many *ie/ei* words, but the following exceptions should be noted:

Exceptions to "i before e"

counterfeit	height	seize
Fahrenheit	heir	sovereign
foreign	leisure	their
forfeit	neither	weird
heifer	protein	

Exceptions to "i before e except after c"

ancient	financier
conscience	proficient
efficient	science

EXERCISE 2.4   *After circling the correctly spelled word, write it in the space under the sentence.*

1. Our team had to (forfeit, forfiet) the game because we didn't have enough players.

   _____

2. Don't eggs contain (protein, protien)?

   _____

3. Ernie is (proficient, proficeint) when it comes to any type of carpentry work.

   _____

4. (Niether, Neither) my parents, siblings nor I smoke.

   _____

5. Did you study any (foreign, foriegn) languages in high school or college?

_____

6. My grandparents seemed (anceint, ancient) when I was growing up, but they were only in their 50's.

_____

7. Biology is the only (science, sceince) course I've had so far, but I've been pursuing my associate's degree for only nine years.

_____

8. What's the difference between Centigrade and (Fahrenhiet, Fahrenheit) thermometer readings?

_____

9. You say you heard some (weird, wierd) noises last night? Well, my dear (neighbor, nieghbor), it was probably my Uncle Roscoe playing his beloved bagpipes.

_____

10. Uncle Roscoe is a bartender at the Belly Up Bar from 4:00 p.m. until midnight, so he can only play his bagpipes in his (leisure, liesure) time, which he says is from 1:00 a.m. until 4:00 a.m. You understand, don't you? He's a very (efficeint, efficient) bagpiper, wouldn't you agree?

_____

11. Did you say Mr. Johnson is an (heir, hier) to another fortune? My goodness, he's already a wealthy (financeir, financier) worth at least $100, wouldn't you say?

_____

12. On Halloween evening, a youngster dressed as a (heifer, hiefer), which caused me to (shreik, shriek) with laughter.

_____

13. My (consceince, conscience) began to bother me as I realized I hadn't taken (suffceient, sufficient) time to help my Aunt Grace can her beets.

_____

✓ CHECK-UP: Chapter 2, -ei and -ie Words

A *Decide whether each word should be spelled with -ei or -ie; then neatly write the entire word on the line before each sentence.*

_____   1. My (n--ghbor) works at the local paper mill.

_____   2. There is a (y--ld) sign at the end of this road.

_____   3. Jackie is a (cash--r) at a café located in the mall.

_____   4. I had a (br--f) conversation with Joey this morning.

_____   5. Morris painted the (c--ling) a shiny white color.

_____   6. Someone let out a terrifying (shr--k) when the lights suddenly went out.

_____ 7. Lola claims she doesn't (w--gh) any more now than she did in high school. (HA!)

_____ 8. Bertie tried to (dec--ve) me by saying he wasn't at home when I called him, but I called him on his smartphone, for crying out loud.

_____ 9. So, naturally, I didn't (bel--ve) him.

_____ 10. So when did you (rec--ve) the news that good old Bertie was engaged?

_____ 11. The trucking company I work for recently bought another massive truck to haul (fr--ght) anywhere in the United States and Canada.

B *One of the five -ei / ie words is misspelled. Circle that word, then neatly spell it correctly in the space provided.*

1.	neice	receipt	quiet	grief	field	_____
2.	rein	cheif	piece	believe	veil	_____
3.	mischief	relief	hygiene	friend	heinous	_____
4.	riegn	thief	sleigh	siege	conceive	_____
5.	conciet	vein	priest	feign	perceive	_____
6.	fierce	achieve	fiend	hier	ancient	_____
7.	sheik	forfeit	neither	sceince	sufficient	_____
8.	weird	handkerchief	financeir	leisure	efficient	_____

Vowel Suffixes

A suffix consists of one or more letters attached to the end of a word, such as *-ed* or *-ing,* borrow<u>ed</u> and borrow<u>ing.</u>

Vowel Suffixes — 1

One useful spelling rule (though wordy) relating to vowel suffixes is this (vowels are represented by *a, e, i, o, u,* and the consonants by all the other letters in the alphabet):

> **GUIDELINE:** When a word ends in a single consonant or is accented on the last syllable, double the final consonant if a vowel suffix is being added.

Examples:

bag	The *-g* is doubled because *bag* ends in a single consonant preceded by a single vowel.	baɢ baɢɢed baɢɢing
permit	The *-t* is doubled because *permit* ends in a single consonant preceded by a single vowel and the accent is on the last syllable (*per MIT*).	permiᴛ permiᴛᴛed permiᴛᴛing
prefer	The *-r* is doubled because *prefer* ends in a single consonant (*r*) preceded by a single vowel (*e*) and the accent is on the last syllable (*pre FER*).	prefeʀ prefeʀʀed prefeʀʀing

Examples of words in which the final consonant is NOT doubled because the conditions of the spelling rule are absent include the following:

bump	The -*p* is NOT doubled because it is preceded by the consonant *m*, not a vowel.	bumP bumPed bumPing
green	The -*n* is NOT doubled because it is preceded by two vowels, not one.	greeN greeNer greeNing
enter	The -*r* is NOT doubled because the accent is on the first syllable (EN ter), not the last one.	enteR enteRed enteRing

---

NOTE: Words beginning with *qu-*, such as quiz, quit, and quiz merit special attention because the *u* is not considered a separate sound but part of a <u>kw</u> or one sound, so the final consonants in these words <u>are</u> doubled when adding a vowel suffix:

> quiz, quizzed, quizzing
> quit, quitting
> quip, quipped, quipping

Transfer, which can serve as either a noun or verb, also deserves special attention as seen in these examples:

- May I get a <u>TRANSfer</u> (noun) to a different bus?
- Please <u>transFER</u> (verb) my call to Mrs. Barker's office.

However, whether *transfer* is accented on the first or last syllable, the *r* is doubled when adding -*ing* or -*ed*:

- Edna's transfe<u>rr</u>ing to the state university was a surprise to me.

She transfe<u>rr</u>ed after her sophomore year.

EXERCISE 3.1 *After circling the correctly spelled word with the vowel suffix, write it in the space provided. <u>Remember,</u> the final consonant of a word is doubled when adding a vowel suffix if the word is of one syllable or ends in a single consonant preceded by a single vowel.*

_____ 1. **dig** — diging / digging

_____ 2. **occur** — occured / occurred

_____ 3. **bright** — brighter / brightter

_____ 4. **quiz** — quizzed / quized

_____ 5. **jog** — jogged / joged

_____ 6. **wrap** — wraping / wrapping

_____ 7. **transfer** — transferred / transfered

_____ 8. **big** — bigger / biger

_____ 9. **drop** — droped / dropped

_____ 10. **jump** — jumping / jumpping

_____ 11. **beg** — begged / beged

_____ 12. **admit** — admitting / admiting

_____ 13. **slam** — slamed / slammed

_____ 14. **quit** — quiting / quitting

_____ 15. **swim** — swiming / swimming

Vowel Suffixes — 2

As has been noted, when a word ends in a single consonant preceded by a single vowel and the word consists of one syllable or is accented on the last syllable, then double the final consonant when adding a vowel suffix:

- bug / buGGed, buGGing
- commit / commiTTed, commiTTing

Therefore, the final consonant of these words should also be doubled because of the preceding rule:

- confer (conFER) / conferred, conferring
- infer (inFER) / inferred, inferring
- prefer (preFER) / preferred, preferring
- refer (reFER) / referred, referring

However, when the vowel suffix is *-ence*, the *r* is NOT doubled because the accent switches to the first syllable:

- confer / CONference
- infer / INference
- prefer / PREference
- refer / REFerence

When adding the vowel suffixes *-ed*, *-ing*, *-able*, *-ive*, and *-ity* to words ending in *-e*, drop the *-e*:

- accuse / accused / accusing
- care / cared / caring
- desire / desired / desiring / desirable
- have / having
- impulse / impulsive
- sincere / sincerity
- write / writing

When adding a vowel suffix to words ending in -ic, add k after the c to maintain the hard c sound:

- frolic / frolicked / frolicking
- mimic / mimicked / mimicking
- panic / panicked / panicking
- picnic / picnicked / picnicking

Also for pronunciation purposes, -ce and -ge words keep the -e when a vowel suffix begins with either -a or -e:

- change / changeable
- courage / courageous
- notice / noticeable
- outrage / outrageous
- peace / peaceable

EXERCISE 3.2 *After circling the correctly spelled word, write it neatly in the space provided. Apply your knowledge of the spelling rules that have been provided in the last two chapters. Check your responses with those in the Answer Key when you are done with this exercise.*

_____ 1. **infer** — infered / inferred

_____ 2. **infer** — inferring / infering

_____ 3. **infer** — inferrence / inference

_____ 4. **notice** — noticed / noticeed

_____ 5. **notice** — noticeing / noticing

_____ 6. **notice** — noticeable / noticable

_____   7. **indulge** — indulgeed / indulged

_____   8. **indulge** — indulgeing / indulging

_____   9. **indulge** — indulgeence / indulgence

_____ 10. **prefer** — preferred / prefered

_____ 11. **prefer**— prefering / preferring

_____ 12. **prefer** — preference / preferrence

_____ 13. **have** — haveing / having

_____ 14. **write** — writing / writeing

_____ 15. **picnic** — picniced / picnicked

_____ 16. **picnic** — picnicing / picnicking

_____ 17. **peace** — peaceable / peacable

_____ 18. **desire** — desireable / desirable

_____ 19. **care** — careing / caring

_____ 20. **panic** — paniccing / panicking

After reviewing Chapter 3, paying particular attention to any items you may have answered incorrectly on the chapter's exercises, do the ***Check-Up*** that follows.

✓ CHECK-UP: Chapter 3, Vowel Suffixes

Apply your knowledge of the spelling rules as they relate to words containing vowel suffixes in the review exercises that follow.

A **Proofread: Circle the correctly spelled word containing a vowel suffix.**

Ginger Snaps

This is the one and only Casper Wilbersnade addressing you again. I'm sure you must remember my heartbreaking story about my former girlfriend Twallah, whose **(1)** (outragous, outrageous) betrayal of me was so devastating, leading to my **(2)** (courageous, couragous) resolve never to date again. However, a cute girl by the name of Ginger Snaps, who is in my ninth grade algebra class, became **(3)** (noticable, noticeable) to me, mainly because of her flaming red hair. My resolve never to date again began to waver. I am **(4)** (writing writeing) to share with you about when my resolve collapsed completely.

As the semester progressed, surprisingly, Ginger never spoke to me though I sat right behind her in class. I finally **(5)** (infered, inferred) that she was **(6)** (ignoring, ignoreing) me because she was overwhelmed by my impressive, but humble, presence.

Then one morning before school started, I noticed Ginger **(7)** (frolicing, frolicking) with "not-a-very-impressive-looking" student named Bozo Rademaker, who had never been privileged to be among my circle of friends. Though I would have **(8)** (prefered, preferred) to talk with Ginger in private, I **(9)** (commited, committed) myself to confronting her at this opportunity.

I boldly said, "Pardon me, Bozo, but I would like a private word with Ginger." Though Bozo ignored what I had said, I decided not to make an issue of it, so I **(10)** (proceeded, proceded) to say, "Ginger, you must know from my outstanding reputation and because I sit behind you in our algebra class, I am the one and only Casper Whipplesnade. Please pardon me for **(11)** (interrupting, interupting) your conversation with Bozo, but after due consideration I have decided to honor you by asking you to go on a date with me this Friday evening, and I am, of course, **(12)** (hopeing, hoping), but quite confident, you will accept." Fortunately, I discovered she wasn't the **(13)** (panicy, panicky) type, but, from all appearances, took my gracious offer in stride.

However, you can well imagine my utter shock when Ginger and Bozo stared at me for what seemed to be an eternity, and then to my absolute embarrassment, started laughing. Ginger finally was able to sputter, "Casper, believe it or not, I already have a date this Friday evening, and it's with Bozo. Besides, I don't think I would find you a **(14)** (desirable, desireable) date in any case."

I finally recovered from my shock and croaked, "What? Are you out of your mind? Why, for heaven's sake? Wouldn't you be ecstatic to go on a date with me? Most girls in their right mind would be thrilled by such an unexpected and glorious opportunity."

Ginger calmly replied, "Frankly, Casper, you're simply much too conceited for me."

Well, that was certainly an uncalled-for statement to make to me, the honorable Casper Whipplesnade, a superlatively gifted but extremely modest person! But, I must admit, there was no **(15)** (escaping, escapeing) Ginger's **(16)** (sincereity, sincerity), the poor misguided creature.

This unpleasant—and, I must confess, shocking—experience, coupled with Twallah's shameless betrayal of me a few weeks earlier, has only deepened once more my resolve to never date, at least in the near future. In fact, I remember making a **(17)** (referrence, reference) in my diary that I would refrain from **(18)** (dateing, dating) forever!

Though I admit in all honesty that I have noticed a cute, vivacious girl in the cafeteria during lunch time. Her name, I **(19)** (discoverred, discovered), is Maxine McGillicuty … but, no, I shall not put myself in a position to be **(20)** (humiliated, humiliateed) once again … even though Maxine looks and acts like a most intelligent girl, one who would no doubt tremble in excitement if I should ask her out on a date … But should I? Ah, what to do, what to do …

B *After circling the correctly spelled word, write it in the space provided.*

_____ 1. Monica is (writing, writting, writeing) a grocery list.

_____ 2. The ashes were still (smokeing, smoking), so I threw some more water and dirt on them.

_____ 3. Is my nose still (bleeding, bleedding)?

_____ 4. Did you attend the (conferrence, conference) on how to raise dandelions?

_____ 5. It's (inconceivable, inconceiveable) to me that you forgot to phone your Aunt Bizinny that we were coming for supper.

_____ 6. Fido has been (waging, wagging) his tail ever since Sweetums the cat let him drink out of her bowl.

_____ 7. Uncle Roger (gulped, gulpped) his drink rapidly, then he erupted with a belch that no doubt could be heard two blocks away.

_____ 8. Nathaniel, are you (fibing, fibbing) to me about the real reason why you lost your job at the Rainbow Club?

_____ 9. Marvelous Marv is (junking, junkking) his 2003 Pontiac.

_____ 10. Yes, those are our cows (grazeing, grazing) in yonder field.

_____ 11. Mrs. Verrill (quizzed, quized) me over an hour about my qualifications for being a shepherd to her large group of prize-winning sheep.

_____ 12. Casanova Carl proved to be a romantic indeed when he (poped, popped) the question to Henrietta, "Will you marry me after we graduate from middle school, my precious darling?"

_____ 13. My dear, sweet, elderly Aunt Wilma said her (preferrence, preference) was a shot of tequila instead of a spot of tea.

_____ 14. Then Uncle Willie proclaimed that he (prefered, preferred) White Lightning to tea.

_____ 15. No passenger (paniced, panicked) during our flight's bumpy ride except for Chicken Little who cried, "The sky is falling! The sky is falling!"

_____ 16. I caught my forty-year-old son Clint (mimicking, mimicing) me in front of his friends, and it was a pretty humorous portrayal of me; nevertheless, I called my lawyer to change my will so that Clint will inherit only fourteen copies of my huge, priceless collection of *Archie* comic books.

_____ 17. The weather has indeed been (changable, changeable) as it rained steadily on Sunday, Monday, and Tuesday, and then hailed lightly on Wednesday; but on Thursday through Saturday it was nothing but blue skies and a brilliant sun.

_____ 18. According to the latest news, a wildfire has been (blazing, blazeing) in the northern part of the state since late last night.

_____ 19. When I was a youngster, I wanted to be a rootin'-tootin' cowboy, but now that I'm a mature adult, my (aspireations, aspirations) include being a stunt driver in Hollywood movies, a lion tamer in a circus, and a brain surgeon in Boston.

_____ 20. My tips at the café have been (ranging, rangeing) from one to twenty dollars.

Prefixes, Compounds, Consonant Suffixes, Final -y Words

4

Prefixes

A <u>prefix</u> is a word part attached <u>before</u> a base word. Common prefixes include *dis-, in-, mis-,* and *un-*. A spelling rule associated with prefixes is to **omit no letters when you join a prefix to a base word:**

dis	+	similar	=	dissimilar
in	+	consistent	=	inconsistent
mis	+	step	=	misstep
un	+	able	=	unable

Compounds

<u>Compound words</u> are two base words combined. The spelling rule associated with compound words is similar to that of joining a prefix to a base word, that is, **when two words are joined to form a compound, omit no letters:**

grand	+	mother	=	grandmother
grass	+	hopper	=	grasshopper
dish	+	washer	=	dishwasher
spear	+	mint	=	spearmint

EXERCISE 4.1 *After circling the correctly spelled word, write it in the space provided.*

_____ 1. Rory's moodiness was (unatural, unnatural) for him.

_____ 2. However, he was obviously (disatisfied, dissatisfied) about something.

_____ 3. Rory eventually told me that someone had smashed his car's (windshield, wind shield) during the night.

_____ 4. Matt bought his wife Jodi an expensive set of (earings, earrings) for their anniversary.

_____ 5. Chauncey, you (misspelled, mispelled) "accidentally" by spelling it "accidently"; do you notice the difference?

_____ 6. My new computer (key board, keyboard) is comfortable to use.

_____ 7. I once was a (sales clerk, salesclerk) at a Sears store in Rutland, Vermont.

_____ 8. Speedster Sylvia will have to be (rexamined, reexamined) before she will be issued a driver's license.

_____ 9. The (sub soil, subsoil) on Uncle Dewey's farm is extremely rich.

_____ 10. Nervous Nesbit, show a little (backbone, back bone) and ask Delores for a date.

Consonant Suffixes

You will recall from Chapter 3 that a <u>suffix</u> is a word part attached at the end of a base word, and that examples of vowel suffixes include *-ed*, *-ing*, *-able*, *-ive*, and *-ity*. A <u>consonant suffix</u>, on the other hand, begins with either *-f*, *-l*, or *m*.

The point to remember is that similar to joining prefixes to a base word or forming a compound word, **consonant suffixes do NOT alter the spelling of the base word**, as seen in the following examples:

base word	+	suffix (-ful)	=	result
care	+	ful	=	careful
cup	+	ful	=	cupful
fright	+	ful	=	frightful
peace	+	ful	=	peaceful

base word	+	suffix (-ly)	=	result
friend	+	ly	=	friendly
quick	+	ly	=	quickly
rapid	+	ly	=	rapidly
slow	+	ly	=	slowly

This spelling rule applies even if the consonant suffix *-ly* is added to a word ending in *-l*:

base word	+	suffix (-ly)	=	result
forceful	+	ly	=	forcefully
hopeful	+	ly	=	hopefully
peaceful	+	ly	=	peacefully
actual	+	ly	=	actually

The suffix *-less* similarly does not alter the spelling of the base word:

base word	+	suffix (-less)	=	result
bottom	+	less	=	bottomless
cease	+	less	=	ceaseless
end	+	less	=	endless
worth	+	less	=	worthless

The same rule applies with the suffix *-ment* as well:

base word	+	suffix (-ment)	=	result
assign	+	ment	=	assignment
confinc	+	ment	=	confinement
develop	+	ment	=	development
pronounce	+	ment	=	pronouncement

Final *-y* Words

As was true of plural nouns ending in *-y* preceded by a consonant (see p. 3), adding suffixes to words ending in *-y* involves **changing the *-y* to *i* IF a consonant precedes the *-y*:**

base word	+	suffix	=	result	notes
beauty	+	ful	=	beautiful	the **-y** in **beauty** is preceded by the consonant **t**, so the **y** is changed to **i** before adding the suffix -**ful**)
glory	+	ous	=	glorious	(the **-y** in **glory** is preceded by the consonant **r**, so the **y** is changed to **i** before adding the suffix -**ous**)
happy	+	ness	=	happiness	(the **-y** is preceded by the consonant **p**, so the **y** is changed to **i** before adding the suffix -**ness**)
pretty	+	est	=	prettiest	(the **-y** is preceded by the consonant **t**, so the **y** is changed to **i** before adding the suffix -**est**)

EXERCISE 4.2 *After underlining the correctly spelled words, check your answers with those in the Answer Key.*

1. Grammy, did you go to many dance (partys, parties) when you were young?

2. My (wristwatch, wrist watch) didn't cost much, but it keeps perfect time.

3. We thought we would be late getting to the airport, but we (actualy, actually) got there in plenty of time.

4. The children's (confinement, confinment) lasted for several weeks because of scarlet fever.

5. Fortunately, the dispute ended (peacefuly, peacefully).

6. The principal made an important (announcement, announcment) regarding the changes being made in the bus routes.

7. My grandfather's (happyness, happiness) appears to depend upon whether there is any ice cream in his house.

8. Brenda (delightfully, delightfuly) gave out the Christmas presents to her many nieces and nephews.

9. Did I (mispell, misspell) the word *committee*?

10. Dan placed the (silverware, silver ware) on the table.

✔ CHECK-UP: Chapter 4, Prefixes, Compounds, Consonant Suffixes, Final -y Words

After reviewing the chapter, complete the following by carefully circling the correctly spelled word in each set of parentheses. Check your answers with those in the Answer Key when you are done.

Deep Death Canyon

Wild Bill said to me, "Are you kidding, Ranger Rick?" Then he continued, "I would **(1)** (absolutly, absolutely) love to trudge through five miles of Deep Death Canyon during the middle of July with Marvelous Marv, Bronco Billy, Hairy Harry, Duplex Dan and you, but, unfortunately, I have a major conflict at that time."

"Which is?" I inquired.

Wild Bill **(2)** (hesitantily, hesitantly) replied, "Ah … let me see … oh, yes, sadly, my high school class reunion is on July 15th."

"Gee, Wild Bill, I didn't know you had graduated from high school." With that "kind" remark Wild Bill and I departed company.

The days dragged by. Marvelous Marv and I and the rest of our Merry Band cheered when July 1st came, and we were **(3)** (practicaly, practically) jumping out of our skin before July 15th arrived, but **(4)** (mercifully, mercifuly), it did. We could **(5)** (finaly, finally) be on our way to Deep Death Canyon!

We just knew we would have many **(6)** (gloryous, glorious) days to look forward to! That fink Wild Bill would eat his heart out with envy when he hears our **(7)** (first hand, firsthand) account of our once-in-a **(8)** (life time, lifetime) great adventure. We knew it would be more thrilling than any **(9)** (amusment, amusement) park we could have gone to.

As I was putting my tent and **(10)** (backpack, back pack)—full of granola bars, bottles of water, suntan lotion, a flashlight, a hammer, a Swiss army knife, a GPS, a tent, a Coleman stove and lantern, my smartphone, a medical kit, and a change of clothes—into the back of my SUV, one of my neighbors, Gloomy Gus, wandered over and frowned, and I said, "Don't be sad, Gloomy Gus. You are still welcome to go with us." I thought for a second or two he was going to throw up, but instead he asked, "Does anyone in your ragtag group have any experience doing challenging hiking? Through the years, there have been a lot of **(11)** (tragedys, tragedies) at Deep Death Canyon, you know."

I laughingly replied, "Yes, I know, Gloomy Gus, but Hairy Harry and Marvelous Marv were in the Boy Scouts for almost a year when they were around twelve years old, so we will do just fine."

Gloomy Gus looked at me and muttered, "Oh brother. Well, it was nice knowing you, Ranger Rick. I hope you and your friends survive so you can live out your other weird **(12)** (fantasies, fantasys)."

On this hot but golden day, our **(13)** (couragous, courageous) group met on the outskirts of town at Larry's Bowling Alley at 9:00 am. We nervously gabbed and giggled for a little while, but we **(14)** (eventualy, eventually) managed to be on our way to Deep Death Canyon by 9:30, **(15)** (traveling, travelling) in Bronco Billy's Jeep and my old but reliable Chevy SUV.

We arrived at the check-in cabin at Deep Death Canyon around noon. We expected to see **(16)** (endless, end less) cars from not only many states but also at least one or two from foreign **(17)** (countrys, countries) as well; however, there were only two other cars besides ours, and they were both from the same state we were from. We expressed our surprise to the check-in clerk about the small number of people registering to go to Deep Death Canyon, and the clerk looked us in the eye and said somewhat **(18)** (accuseingly, accusingly), "Unlike some weirdos, it's because most people are too smart to go hiking in 100-plus temperatures." "Well," I thought, "the more likely reason is because most people don't have the gumption or sense of adventure my **(19)** (buddies, buddys) and I have." **(20)** (Actually, Actualy), we were fortunate in a way that there were such few people at the entrance to Deep Death Valley because we had our choice of a couple of lean-tos, so we were spared the work of **(21)** (puting, putting) up our tents.

After cooking hotdogs and ears of corn on our Coleman stove and slurping lemonade, we **(22)** (wearily, wearyly) struggled to lie down in our uncomfortable lean-tos for the night. However, none of us, except Hairy Harry, slept much because of our sleep **(23)** (enemies, enemys), which included the heat, humidity, mosquitoes, the **(24)** (crudness, crudeness) of the lean-tos, and, certainly not least, Hairy Harry's blaring snoring.

Despite little sleep, everyone was in a surprisingly **(25)** (up beat, upbeat) mood in the morning, and after a breakfast of **(26)** (pancakes, pan cakes) topped by real Maine maple syrup, bacon, orange juice, and coffee, we were eager to conquer Deep Death Canyon. Give us your best shot DDC! We put on our backpacks and our wide brim hats, and off we went, following the signs to where hikers were directed to enter.

We were so proud of ourselves for daring to tackle this challenging adventure, thanks to the brilliant Marvelous Marv, whose idea it was, along with mine, of course. We all laughingly burst out in song, singing "Ho! Ho! It's off to a great time we go!"

Soon, however, after enduring the **(27)** (ceaseless, ceasless) sun beating down on us for almost an hour, our shirts were soaked with sweat, and we felt miserable and **(28)** (power less, powerless), not only because of the scorching sun and the **(29)** (relentless, relent less) flies and mosquitoes, but also because we had forgotten to put on any **(30)** (sun screen, sunscreen) in the morning, so our arms, lower legs and necks were now an unattractive shade of red, not to mention that these body parts were **(31)** (already, all ready) **(32)** (painfully, painfuly) stiff and sore.

In addition, our feet throbbed with pain because we were wearing new L.L. Bean hiking boots **(33)** (without, with out) breaking them in before going on this ill-advised trip (thanks to good old stupid Marvelous Marv, because this trip was all his big idea, the fool!). In fact, our feet were now so sore we considered going **(34)** (barefoot, bare foot), but one **(35)** (foot print, footprint) on the trail's scalding hot sand quickly put the kabosh on this idea. Most alarmingly of all, though, we each had already drunk over half of the water in our canteens.

We still needed to hike over a half mile to reach Deep Death Canyon's floor, and some of us started complaining of **(36)** (dizzyness, dizziness). Suddenly, Bronco Billy let out a terrifying screech. "What's wrong, Bronco Billy?" I **(37)** (panicly, panickly) asked.

In response, he gargled, "Look—there!" as he pointed to a large boulder. "What the …" Then we all saw what Bronco Billy was pointing at—a large **(38)** (rattlesnake, rattle snake) curled up near the front end of the boulder, along with a couple of **(39)** (grasshoppers, grass hoppers) **(40)** (lazily, lazyly) sunning **(41)** (them selves, themselves) **(42)** (nearby, near by).

"Yikes," I said, "let's get out of here!" and we tore back up the trail as fast as our sore feet, tired legs, **(43)** (sunburned, sun burned) skin, and thirsty souls would carry us. It wasn't that we didn't have any **(44)** (back bone, backbone), you understand, we just didn't want to upset the snake as it looked so comfortable where it was lying.

When we got back to our lean-tos, we quickly decided to head home and back to civilization, as Deep Death Canyon's "charms" had evaporated as far as we were concerned. After all, we had been here for almost twenty-four hours, so no one could ever question our courage and staying-power in the face of terrifying obstacles. So we quickly threw our belongings in the cars and sped back to the **(45)** (highway, high way) that would take us home, sweet home.

After an hour or so, we had calmed down enough to stop at a **(46)** (restaurant, restaraunt) called the Last Gasp Café located just beyond an **(47)** (over pass, overpass). After refreshing **(48)** (ourselves, our selves) in the **(49)** (rest room, restroom) and gobbling cheeseburgers, a platter of onion rings, pieces of strawberry pie, and a couple of cans of root beer **(50)** (apiece, a piece), we felt much better and were in good spirits as we resumed our trip back home. We vowed to tell Wild Bill and Gloomy Gus that "You should have been with us!" We had a blast **(51)** (relating, relateing) our life and death struggle with the largest rattlesnake ever seen by anyone who lived to tell it, pointing out that **(52)** (human kind, humankind) was not meant to deal with such monsters, but we brave souls had the gumption to do so, refusing to back down to a snake or any other furious creature.

However, we also agreed that the only adventures we would be going on in the near future would be to dances or birthday **(53)** (parties, partys) with our wives, since it is **(54)** (un likely, unlikely) we could ever again duplicate the bravery we displayed at Deep Death Canyon.

Words Frequently Confused – 1

Words can be confused with one another because they sound the same, so spelling mistakes are common with such words. However, this chapter and the one that follows provide you with an opportunity to permanently avoid misspelling (and misunderstanding) these words.

SET A

1. **a, an**

   <u>A</u> is used before words beginning with a consonant:

   > Do you need a <u>r</u>ide to work?
   > > (<u>r</u> *of* ride *is a consonant, so* **a** *is used before it*)

   <u>An</u> is used before words beginning with a vowel that is, *a, e, i, o, u*:

   > An <u>a</u>irplane could be heard in the distance.
   > > (<u>a</u> *of* airplane *is a vowel, so* **an** *is used before it*)

2. **accept, except**

   <u>Accept</u> means "to receive":

   > Belinda will **accept** the award on behalf of her daughter who, unfortunately, is sick with the measles.

   <u>Except</u> means "all but":

   > Everyone will be attending the family reunion this weekend **except** Uncle Grumpus.

3. **advice, advise**

   <u>Advice</u> is a *noun* meaning a suggestion or an opinion:

   > My **advice** is for you to look for a summer job no later than the first of April.

   <u>Advise</u> is a *verb* that means to offer a suggestion or an opinion:

   > I also think Dr. Artesani would **advise** you to look for a summer job related to your college major.

4. **affect, effect**

   <u>Affect</u> is a *verb* that means to influence:

   > Exercise can **affect** your health in many positive ways.

   <u>Effect</u> is a *noun* that means a "result":

   > One positive **effect** of exercise includes having more energy.

5. **brake, break**

   <u>Brake</u> as a *noun* is a device used for slowing down or stopping a car or some other object:

   > Natasha said the front **brake** on her bike isn't working.

   <u>Brake</u> as a *verb* refers to the act of slowing down or stopping an object:

   > The pilot quickly started to **brake** the plane as it taxied down the runway after landing.

   <u>Break</u> means to crack or to smash something to pieces:

   > Be careful you guys don't **break** a window kicking that soccer ball around.

   <u>Break</u> can also refer to surpassing a limit or record:

   > The coach thinks Teresa could **break** the school's 400 meter record at Friday's track meet.

   A third meaning of **break** is to stop an activity to rest or refresh oneself:

   > We took a **break** from studying to play a few games of ping-pong.

6. **breath, breathe**

Breath is a *noun* referring to inhaling and exhaling:

> Jodi took a big **breath** before singing her solo.

Breathe is a *verb* referring to the taking in and out of air into the lungs:

> As we ascended the mountain, it became more difficult to **breathe**.

7. **capital, capitol**

Capital can refer to the city where the official seat of a state's or country's government is located:

> Trenton is the **capital** city of New Jersey; Madrid is the **capital** city of Spain.

Capital may also refer to the large letters that begin the names of books, songs, cities, states, and many other major words:

> Make sure to use a **capital** T when writing Tallahassee.

In addition, capital can refer to wealth in the form of money or property:

> My uncles were able to build their restaurant a number of years ago after using their homes for collateral in securing the necessary **capital** for the structure.

On the other hand, capitol (notice the o instead of a) refers to the major official building where government work is carried out.

> Our state's **Capitol** Building is undergoing some much-needed repairs.

8. **cloths, clothes**

Cloths is a *noun* referring to fabrics such as cotton and wool:

> The **cloths** in this quilt were given to me by my grandmother.

Clothes is a *noun* referring to garments or dress worn:

> Byron appears to wear new **clothes** every week.

EXERCISE 5.1   *After studying each sentence, circle the appropriate word in parentheses.*

1. The movie was so scary I could hardly (breath, breathe), but I finally could take a (breath, breathe) after what seemed like (a, an) eternity.

2. Winning the state high school basketball championship had (a, an) positive (affect, effect) on everyone in our small community; did it (affect, effect) you in any way, Uncle Barnabas?

3. Zell, it's wonderful you had enough (capital, capitol) to pay cash for a sparkling new suit; now you can enter the state (capital, capitol) building in style.

4. Okay, so if you won't (accept, except) (a, an) penny for your thoughts, then how about (a, an) i.o.u. for a dime?

5. If you don't pump your (brakes, breaks) on your bike going down Oak Street Hill, you might (brake, break) a number of bones in your body.

6. Aunt Delores is looking for old pieces of (clothes, cloths) suitable for dusting. She's also planning to alter some of Audry's (cloths, clothes) so they will fit Audry's younger sister.

7. Did Tony (advice, advise) you to wait until the temperature was higher before painting your garage? If so, his (advice, advise) was sound, so don't you think you should follow it?

EXERCISE 5.2 *Write original sentences for the following words that clearly demonstrates your understanding of their meaning and spelling. Have a qualified person check your work.*

1. capitol _____

_____

2. capital _____

_____

3. cloths _____

_____

4. clothes _____

_____

5. advice _____

_____

6. advise _____

_____

7. accept _____

_____

8. except _____

_____

9. breath _____ _____

_____

10. breathe _____

_____

11. a _____

_____

12. an _____

_____

13. brake _____

_____

14. break _____

_____

15. affect _____

_____

16. effect _____

_____

SET B

1. **desert, dessert**

   <u>Desert</u> as a *noun* (with accent on the first syllable) refers to (1) a dry, barren land.

   > Much of North Africa is a **desert**.

   But <u>desert</u> as a *verb* (accenting the second syllable) can also refer to (2) the forsaking of one's duty.

   > Tad, don't **desert** your post because someone may wander too close to the edge of the cliff.

   <u>Dessert</u> is usually the last food, such as ice cream or pie, served at a meal (notice that there are two *s*'s in des-SERT).

   > Marcella served angel food cake with whipped cream for **dessert**.

2. **device, devise**

   <u>Device</u> refers to an object:

   > This little gadget is a handy **device** for opening cans and bottles.

   <u>Devise</u> refers to developing a plan, strategy, or solution:

   > Our city's engineering department needs to **devise** a solution for our street's flooding problem we often have during the rainy season.

3. **eminent, imminent**

   <u>Eminent</u> describes something that (or someone who) is famous, noteworthy, or distinguished:

   > Sherlock Holmes is probably the most **eminent** person living in our community, but Batman runs him a close second.

   <u>Imminent</u> describes something that is about to happen:

   > A rainstorm is **imminent** as it has become dark and windy, and thunder can be heard in the distance.

4. **farther, further**

   <u>Farther</u> refers to physical distance:

Her hometown is located twenty-six miles **farther** north of our present location.

Further indicates to a greater degree or extent:
> The spokesperson said the proposal to expand the company's plant requires **further** study before a final decision is reached.

5. **forth, fourth**
Forth is concerned with what is happening or what is to occur:
> From that day **forth**, Sandra never missed a day of school.

Fourth is concerned with the number four:
> We live in the **fourth** largest city in the state.

6. **hole, whole**
Hole is a cavity or an opening through something:
> Did you know there is a **hole** in your sweater?

Whole means "complete" or "entire":
> Glory me! Did you eat the **whole** pizza by yourself?

7. **its, it's**
Its is a possessive pronoun; that is, its indicates ownership of something:
> Our old tractor is on **its** last legs.

It's with an apostrophe is a contraction for "it is" or "it has":
- Did you know **it's** Halloween tomorrow night?
- Noah, **it's** been raining for forty days and forty nights; now what are we going to do?

8. **loose, lose**
Loose (with the "s" pronounced normally) means "free, unrestrained":
> Our dog got **loose** when someone left the back door unshut.

<u>Lose</u> (with the "s" pronounced like a "z") means (1) to be defeated:
> I hope my favorite team doesn't **lose** in the playoffs.

or (2) to misplace something:
> Maynard, did you **lose** your car keys again?

EXERCISE 5.3 *After studying each sentence, circle the appropriate word in parentheses.*

1. Unquestionably, Miss Mallory Wiggins, the owner of the Speedy Diner on River Street, is the most (eminent, imminent) person living in our neighborhood, and I think wider fame is (eminent, imminent) for Miss Wiggins as she's going to have a cooking show on our local TV station.

2. Does anyone have a wrench? The handlebars on my bike are (lose, loose).

3. Ross said that someday he's going to ride his motorcycle across the Mojave (Desert, Dessert).

4. Ross (farther, further) said he was going to ride his motorcycle from San Diego to the very end of South America.

5. (Its, It's) just like Ross to make such claims as he's made such boasts his (hole, whole) life.

6. This (devise, device) is a musical instrument? Really? Who's the mastermind that (deviced, devised) it? This so-called instrument looks like a car's tailpipe.

7. "Go (forth, fourth) and sin no more!" the pastor shouted.

8. This faucet has lost (its, it's) water power.

9. My Uncle Biggie, who races in a beat up old Chevy, brags that he finished (forth, fourth) at Wimpy's Speedway last Saturday night. I learned later that there were only four cars competing in that particular race.

10. You have two choices for (dessert, desert): one stale cracker or, if you prefer, two stale crackers.

11. Bert exclaimed, "Oh, no! There is a large (hole, whole) in the sleeve of my new jacket!"

12. "Batman would never (desert, dessert) the citizens of Gotham City in their time of need!" Robin insisted.

13. Just then, a cat strolled across the sidewalk, so I had to (break, brake) my tricycle to avoid hitting it.

| EXERCISE 5.4 | *Write original sentences for the following words that clearly demonstrate you understand their meaning as well as their spelling. When you have finished, have a qualified person check your work.* |

1. farther _____

_____

2. loose _____

_____

3. its _____

_____

4. devise _____

_____

5. imminent _____

_____

6. fourth _____

_____

7. dessert _____

_____

8. further _____

_____

9. eminent _____

_____

10. forth _____

_____

11. device _____

_____

12. desert (two sentences indicating its two meanings)

_____

_____

_____

13. whole _____

_____

14. lose _____

_____

15. it's _____

_____

16. hole _____

_____

17. break (three sentences indicating its three meanings)

_____

_____

_____

_____

✔ CHECK-UP: Chapter 5, Words Frequently Confused – 1

After studying each sentence, circle the appropriate word, and then write it on the line provided.

1. What (advice, advise) would you give me about how to get a job like yours?

   _____

2. My nephew will be in (forth, fourth) grade this fall.

   _____

3. I finally have enough (capital, capitol) to open (a, an) ice cream shop, something I've been dreaming about for years.

   _____

4. Could you (device, devise) a way to water my garden without using this leaking hose?

   _____

5. Well, rain seems (eminent, imminent), so that should solve your problem.

   _____

6. By the way, before irrigation, this (hole, whole) area was a (desert, dessert).

   _____

7. I'm going to change into some cooler (cloths, clothes) as (its, it's) becoming hot and humid.

   _____

8. Rosie needs a wrench to tighten a (loose, lose) bolt on her wheelbarrow.

   _____

9. Bernie said he likes everything about this part of the country (accept, except) the climate, people, and government.

   _____

10. I'm going to (brake, break) up with my
    boyfriend if I don't (loose, lose) my nerve as
    well as my (breath, breathe).   _____

11. Alberto, I (advice, advise) you to stop teasing
    my dog.   _____

12. Camilla asked the waiter, "What else do you
    have for (desert, dessert) besides ice cream and
    pig knuckles?"   _____

13. To make a smooth, gradual stop, press gently on
    the (break, brake) pedal.   _____

14. On behalf of Billy Butterfingers, I (accept,
    except) this trophy for the all-time record for
    making errors by a shortstop.   _____

15. George talks so fast I don't understand how he
    can (breath, breathe).   _____

16. The (capital, capitol) building is open even
    on holidays.   _____

17. This dog blanket was made by sewing together
    old rags and other (cloths, clothes).   _____

18. (A, An) sales person is at the door who would
    like to sell us (a, an) (device, devise) for killing
    flies. He says (its, it's) called a "fly swatter," and
    (its, it's) color is a striking orange.   _____

19. How did the wonderful news (affect, effect) Uncle Bob? I'd think it would have a super (affect, effect) on him.

    _____

20. The much-admired mayor is an (eminent, imminent) person in our community, but I wish her voice would go (forth, fourth) with more vigor when she talks.

    _____

21. How much (farther, further) is it to the ski lodge? Did the storekeeper give you any (farther, further) news about a possible avalanche in this area?

    _____

22. That pothole is the largest (hole, whole) I've seen since I was at the Grand Canyon a couple of years ago.

    _____

Words Frequently Confused – 2

SET A

1. **plain, plane**

   Plain means easily understood or unadorned:
   - Maude's directions were so **plain** that even I couldn't have gotten lost.
   - Our motel room was quite **plain** as it contained just the barest essentials.

   Plane refers to an aircraft:

   My eighty-year old grandfather took his first **plane** ride this week when he flew to Buffalo.

   Plane can also refer to a tool used to smooth wood:

   Merle is using a **plane** to smooth down these rough boards.

2. **principal, principle**

   Principal refers to the main or chief one:

   The **principal** reason Jenna dumped Bubba was because he was constantly biting his nails.

   Principal can also refer to a school administrator:

   Did you know that Harold's wife was the **principal of** Johnson Middle School?

   Principal can relate to financial matters as well:

   I should have enough **principal** when I cash in my stocks and bonds to pay cash for a condo in Vancouver, British Columbia.

   Principle refers to a rule or standard:

   A good **principle** to follow is to always get to work on time.

3. **quit, quiet, quite**

 <u>Quit</u> means to stop or discontinue:

   Marcel **quit** his morning paper route a few days ago.

 <u>Quiet</u> is associated with silence or peacefulness:

   The house was finally **quiet** after the dog, cat, canary, and children went to bed.

 <u>Quite</u> means completely, utterly, or impressively:

   Sue is not only an outstanding banjo player, but she is also **quite** a talented quilter of colorful bedspreads.

4. **shone, shown**

 <u>Shone</u> is the past tense of the verb *shine:*

   Only a single street light **shone** on the narrow, dark street.

 <u>Shown</u> is the past participle of the verb *show:*

   The movie will be shown again at 9:30 p.m.

5. **than, then**

 <u>Than</u> is used in comparisons:

   The swimming pool was more crowded today **than** it was yesterday.

 <u>Then</u> refers to *when* or *at that time:*

   After a snack, Grover yawned, **then** he went to bed.

6. **their, there, they're**

 <u>Their</u> is a possessive pronoun, meaning *belonging to them:*

   Their plan is to drive 500 miles a day until they reach Sacramento.

 <u>There</u> refers to a place or is used to point out something:

   The restaurant **there** across from the park is popular with people of all ages.

   Over **there** on the floor next to the door is somebody's wallet.

 <u>They're</u> is a contraction for *they are:*

   I know **they're** planning to buy a house next summer.

7. **threw, through**

 <u>Threw</u> is the past tense of the verb *throw:*

Louise **threw** a bag of old newspapers and magazines in the recycle barrel.

Through means *from one side to the other*:

It was a little eerie to drive **through** that long tunnel in the middle of the night.

Through can also mean *completed*:

We got **through** painting the garage by the middle of the afternoon.

8. **to, too, two**

To generally introduces an infinitive phrase, which is made up of *to* plus a verb:

Mariah plans **to** jog on Mondays, Wednesdays, and Fridays.

To can also introduce a prepositional phrase; such a phrase is formed when a noun is added to a preposition:

The election outcome was like a tonic **to** Tom.

Too means *also*:

Like Freddie, I'm looking for a job, **too.**

Too can also mean *more than enough*:

We've had **too** much rain this spring, so there is a danger of flooding.

Two refers to the numeral 2:

There were only **two** other people in the theater when we got there.

EXERCISE 6.1 *After studying each sentence, neatly circle the appropriate word in parentheses.*

1. When Jackson was (threw, through) reading the (to, too, two) magazines, he (than, then) (threw, through) them over (to, too, two) me as he knew I wanted (to, too, two) read them (to, too, two).

2. My grandparents live on Walnut Street, and they have lived (their, there, they're) in (their, there, they're) home for over forty years as (their, there, they're) very happy (their, there, they're).

3. It was (quit, quiet, quite) after my roommate finally (quit, quiet, quite) snoring, which had lasted for (quit, quiet, quite) some time.

4. Maria Martinez is the (principal, principle) of the elementary school that my son attends. A (principal, principle) of hers is to greet as many children as she can when they arrive at school each morning.

5. The sun (shone, shown) brilliantly as I was (shone, shown) to my seat in the bleachers.

6. Casper (than, then) said, "Everyone I know seems to think Bozo Rademaker is a fine person, so perhaps I should reevaluate him as I would rather change my mind (than, then) be wrong about him."

7. My glasses, I embarrassingly discovered, were in (plain, plane) sight, so after I put them on I was able to walk down the aisle of the (plain, plane) without stumbling in to one of the airline attendants, who were wearing (plain, plane) blue suits.

EXERCISE 6.2 *Write original sentences for the following words that clearly demonstrate your mastery of their spelling as well as their meaning. When you are finished, have a qualified person check your work.*

1. than _____

_____

2. quit _____

_____

3. principle _____

_____

4. two _____

_____

5. plane _____

_____

6. then _____

_____

7. quite _____

_____

8. threw _____

_____

9. plain _____

_____

10. their _____

_____

11. too _____

_____

12. shone _____

_____

13. quiet _____

_____

14. shown _____

_____

15. through _____

_____

16. principal _____

_____

17. they're _____

_____

18. there _____

_____

19. than _____

SET B

1. **coarse, course**
   <u>Coarse</u> is an *adjective* used to describe something that is rough or vulgar:
   - It will obviously take a lot of **coarse** sandpaper to smooth out the top of this old desk.
   - Despite the constant troubles we experienced during our vacation, I'm proud to say none of us ever used **coarse** language at any time to express our frustrations.

   <u>Course</u> is a *noun* that can refer to a plan, route, or academic subject:
   - The county supervisor's **course** of action is to immediately seek state and federal financial help to replace the unsafe bridge on outer Willow Street.
   - Follow the **course** I've outlined for you on this map and you'll be in Sugar Grove in an hour or so.
   - Rachel says she is enjoying her geometry **course.**

2. **complement, compliment**
   <u>Complement</u> is something that completes or brings to perfection:
   The green shutters will certainly **complement** the house's white vinyl siding.
   <u>Compliment</u> is to commend or to praise:
   Sydney, I would like to **compliment** you on your excellent work.

3. **conscience, conscious**
   <u>Conscience</u> refers to a person's sense of right or wrong:
   Sheridan's **conscience** began to bother him as he recalled how rude he had been to his sister at breakfast.
   <u>Conscious</u> refers to being awake, alert or aware:
   The patient was **conscious** soon after the surgery.

4. **passed, past**
   <u>Passed</u> is the past tense of the verb *pass*:

We **passed** several restaurants before finally stopping to eat at Charlie Chuck's Cafe.

Past is a noun that relates to a previous time:

In the **past**, most of this part of the state was farmland.

5. **personal, personnel**

Personal refers to private matters:

No one in the family, as far as I know, has ever asked Uncle Frank why he and Aunt Betty got divorced, because that is too **personal** of a question.

Personnel refers to a group of people working for the same organization:

The **personnel** at the Outlaw Bank and Chicken Hatchery are all quite friendly, including the chief officers, Mr. Jesse James and Mrs. Fluffy Henfeathers.

6. **weather, whether**

Weather is concerned with atmospheric conditions, such as air temperature and wind speed:

The state of Washington's **weather** is ideal for the growing of apples.

Whether expresses doubt or a choice between alternatives:

I'm not sure **whether** I should buy or lease a car; what do you think I should do?

7. **wear, where**

Wear (*wear, wore, worn*) has to do with clothes:

I've never seen Brian **wear** anything but jeans and a polo shirt.

Wear can also refer to the reduction of something because of overexposure or overuse:

The tires on my car are beginning to show a lot of **wear.**

Where is related to a place:

Where in the world is Villisca?

8. **your, you're**

Your is a possessive pronoun:

Is that **your** bicycle leaning against the house?

You're is a contraction standing for *you are*:

Did you say **you're** taking guitar lessons?

EXERCISE 6.3 *After studying the sentence, circle the appropriate word.*

1. (Weather, Whether) the (weather, whether) is good or bad, the Kincaids say they are leaving tomorrow morning on a trip to visit their relatives in Kansas, including Dorothy and her dog Toto.

2. In the (passed, past) when my son was a pre-teenager, we often (passed, past) the time by shooting baskets or bows and arrows.

3. Dino is interested in taking a (coarse, course) in Chinese history.

4. Do you happen to know (wear, where) Roberta bought her car?

5. Apparently, our supervisor's (conscience, conscious) seldom bothers him, so I'm not surprised he hasn't apologized to you and the others for his critical remarks.

6. (Your, You're) fortunate to get home before the storm came.

7. The player was momentarily stunned, but he's fully (conscience, conscious) now.

8. Do you think this blouse will (complement, compliment) the skirt I'm wearing?

9. Does (your, you're) dog ever make a mess in (your, you're) house, or is that too (personal, personnel) of a question?

10. Mr. Bonner is the only person I know who can (wear, where) a bow tie and not look ridiculous.

11. This golf (coarse, course) may be difficult, Buddy, but that's no excuse for using (coarse, course) language after every shot.

12. Buddy, I'd like to (complement, compliment) you on cleaning up your language after I spoke to you about it. The teaching pro and the rest of the club's (personal, personnel) will be delighted to hear that you have improved (your, you're) language.

✓ CHECK-UP: Chapter 6, Frequently Confused Words – 2

A *After studying each sentence, neatly circle the correct word or words.*

1. After Thor was discharged from the Marines, he (than, then) attended a college in Fullerton, California.

2. I think (your, you're) white walls (complement, compliment) (your, you're) blue sofa, so I (complement, compliment) you on (your, you're) good fashion taste.

3. Vicki quickly (threw, through) her jacket in the passenger seat before driving (threw, through) one of Pennsylvania's long interstate tunnels.

4. Do you think the (weather, whether) is (to, too, two) bad for the (to, too, two) of us (to, too, two) play golf?

5. (Weather, Whether) or not you (wear, where) a tie doesn't really matter because (wear, where) we're going you'll see people of all ages dressed formally, such as Count Dracula, and informally, such as Harry Hobo.

6. The (quit, quiet, quite) environment (wear, where) I work is something I appreciate, so I'm not planning to (quit, quiet, quite) my job any time soon, particularly because my colleagues are (quit, quiet, quite) nice.

7. Ralph Caruthers and Bruce Witherspoon have been trying to reach you, so I wrote down (their, there, they're) phone numbers on a piece of paper, which is (their, there, they're) on (your, you're) desk. (Their, There, They're) (quit, quiet, quite) eager to talk to you, that was (quit, quiet, quite) obvious.

8. I told Ralph and Bruce that (your, you're) usually home by now, but that sometimes (your, you're) job requires you to work later (than, then) usual. I offered to take a message, but the information they wish to share with you was (to, too, two) (personal, personnel) to share with anyone but you.

9. I'm not (conscience, conscious) of any problem they might be having in the (personal, personnel) office where Ralph and Bruce both work. I'll call them back right now before any more time has (passed, past). In the (passed, past) whenever Ralph or Bruce has called me, it was important, so I don't want my (conscience, conscious) to bother me, so please hand me the phone—but wait a minute while I take off the sweater I'm (wearing, whereing) because (its, it's) (coarse, course) material makes me itch.

10. Paul, are you (conscience, conscious) of the fact that we have a (plain, plane) to catch early tomorrow morning? (Its, It's) (plain, plane) to see you haven't even started to pack (your, you're) suitcase.

11. After we were (shone, shown) our seats in the theater, my little daughter's face (shone, shown) with delight.

Spelling Challenges – 1

When we speak to others, we likely slur or omit certain letters; perhaps, for example, we might say *accidently* instead of *accidentally* or *choclate* instead of *chocolate.*

Slurring or omitting letters when we talk usually doesn't create a problem because the people we're talking to can ask us for clarification, and, in addition, our gestures and tone of voice often contribute to what we're saying. Also, paradoxically, if we slow down our speech to make sure we pronounce every letter in every word distinctly, our communication would likely be frustrating to us as well as to our listeners.

However, when we communicate through writing, we need to include all letters in a word, so we should take the time to pronounce fully each syllable of a word, particularly those that are often slurred or those in which an *-e* is dropped. Again, you may find the *Three-W Steps Method* listed in the Introduction helpful for mastering the spelling of those words you find particular challenging. For your convenience, the steps are listed below:

1. _WRITE_   *the word in large script;*
2. _WRITE_   *the word in the air with your eyes shut;*
3. _WRITE_   *the word on paper; check to make sure you have spelled the word correctly.*

Each of the following frequently used words has the part underlined where spelling errors most often appear, and after the word in parentheses is the number of syllables in this word because pronouncing each syllable as you spell the word can contribute to its correct spelling.

Other suggestions relating to the spelling of these words are also included.

SET A

word	syllables	notes
1. amat<u>eu</u>r	3	When **amateur** is misspelled, it's usually because the **-eu** has been reversed.
2. bound<u>a</u>ry	3	Many people say or write "boundry"; correctly pronouncing it will help you to spell **bound<u>a</u>ry** correctly.
3. di<u>a</u>lect	3	Check the number of syllables in **di<u>a</u>lect**; its correct spelling will likely result if you keep the second syllable in mind.
4. li<u>a</u>ble	3	Note the word **-able** appears in **li<u>a</u>ble**.
5. mini<u>a</u>ture	4	Pronounce each syllable of **mini<u>a</u>ture** and you likely will not omit the **-a** in the third syllable.
6. parli<u>a</u>ment	4	**Parliament** is another word that is frequently misspelled because of an omitted **-a**.
7. prob<u>a</u>bly	3	**Probably** has three syllables, but the second one is frequently slurred when the word is spoken, and this slurring is sometimes carried over when it is written, resulting in "probly"—so you may want to pronounce **probably** slowly to yourself when you spell it.
8. quand<u>a</u>ry	3	As is true of **bound<u>a</u>ry**, the same is true of **quand<u>a</u>ry**, that is, pronouncing each syllable makes it less likely you'll leave out the **-a** as so many people do.
9. temper<u>a</u>ment	4	Again, if you pronounce each of the syllables in **temperament**, you likely will spell it correctly because you won't be tripped up by the **-a** in the third syllable.
10. valu<u>a</u>ble	4	I suspect—or hope—you have noticed that **-a** is the key to spelling many of the words in this list.

11.	accident<u>ally</u>	5	*You will almost certainly spell the next five words correctly if you pronounce them appropriately, making sure you pronounce the -**ally** at the end of each one.*
12.	basic<u>ally</u>	4	*See the comment for #11.*
13.	coincident<u>ally</u>	6	*See the comment for #11.*
14.	incident<u>ally</u>	5	*See the comment for #11.*
15.	practic<u>ally</u>	4	*You guessed it—see the comment for #11.*
16.	a<u>c</u>quaint	2	*The **c** in **a<u>c</u>quaint** may be silent, but it belongs in this word as it does in the following three words.*
17.	a<u>c</u>quire	2	*See the comment for #16.*
18.	a<u>c</u>qui<u>tt</u>al	3	*The **c** in **a<u>c</u>quittal** is also silent, but don't forget to include it when you spell this word; notice also the two **t's** and the short word **quit** in **acquittal**.*
19.	ar<u>c</u>tic	2	*Many people do not pronounce the first **c** in **arctic**, leading to its omission when the word is spelled.*
20.	criti<u>c</u>ism	4	*The underlined **c**, which has an "s" sound in this instance, is often omitted in the spelling of **criti<u>c</u>ism**; this error can be avoided if one remembers that **critic** begins this word.*
21.	tragedy	3	*This is a challenging word to spell because it's often pronounced and spelled as "tradegy"— but don't you be one of those people!*

EXERCISE 7.1 *In the space provided, write "correct" if the word is spelled correctly; if the word is misspelled, write its correct spelling.*

1. accidently _____

2. criticism _____

3. valueable   _____

4. aquire   _____

5. artic   _____

6. boundry   _____

7. dialect   _____

8. incidentally   _____

9. parliment   _____

10. coincidently   _____

11. tradegy   _____

12. aquaint   _____

13. miniture   _____

14. practilly   _____

15. basiclly   _____

16. quandry   _____

17. amateur   _____

18. temperament   _____

19. probly   _____

20. lible   _____

21. aquitial   _____

SET B

word	syllables	notes
1. can<u>d</u>idate	3	*The common error in spelling **candidate** is omitting the first -d. As you can see, **candidate** consists of three short words: **can-did-ate**, so this fact may help you to spell this word.*
2. gran<u>d</u>father	3	*You might say "granfather," but there is a -d in **grandfather**. So be sure to put grand+father together when you spell this word.*
3. gran<u>d</u>mother	3	*The comments made about spelling **grand+father** (#2), also apply to **grandmother**.*
4. san<u>d</u>wich	2	*Again, pronunciation is important to the spelling of **sandwich** as many people say and spell this word with the -d missing—"sanwich."*
5. bach<u>e</u>lor	3	***Bachelor** has three syllables, so be sure to include the second one: -e.*
6. exe<u>rc</u>ise	3	*Don't forget the -c after the -r in **exercise**.*
7. math<u>e</u>matics	4	*The second syllable of **mathematics** has an "uh" sound, which in this case is represented by **e**, NOT **a**.*
8. o<u>cc</u>a<u>s</u>ion	3	*This is a challenging word to spell because pronouncing **occasion** correctly isn't too helpful in spelling it. Instead, focus on the twin -c's and the single -s to master the spelling of **occasion**.*
9. pun<u>c</u>tuation	4	*The key to spelling **punctuation** correctly is the -c— don't forget it!*
10. bus<u>i</u>ness	3	*Note that the -i is not pronounced in **business**, but don't leave it out when you spell it. This word is related to "busyness."*
11. cho<u>c</u>olate	3	*Paying attention to **chocolate**'s correct pronunciation is the key to spelling it correctly.*

12. discipline	3	*Note the two **i**'s; the only **-e** in **discipline** comes at the end. Also note the **-c** is silent.*
13. occurrence	3	*Note the twin **c**'s and twin **r**'s in **occurrence**.*
14. dilemma	3	*Remembering the name of **Emma** can help you spell **dilemma**.*
15. recommend	3	*Yep, there is only <u>one</u> **-c** but <u>two</u> **-m**'s in **recommend**.*
16. recognize	3	***Recognize** is a spelling challenge for many people, with some spelling it "reconize," "reccagnise" or some such variation; however, remembering that the small word **-cog-** appears in the middle, and that the last syllable is spelled **-nize**, will likely help you to spell **recognize** correctly.*
17. environment	4	*Remember **-iron-** appears in **environment**; this will prevent you from spelling it as "envirment" or "enviroment."*
18. sophomore	3	*Notice that the **-o** in the middle of **sophomore** is the second of three syllables in this word. It's probably okay if you <u>say</u> "sophmore," but when you spell it, make sure you have **-o** after the **-h**!*
19. congratulate	4	*Notice that the second syllable of **congratulate** ends in **-t** not **-d**.*
20. quantity	3	*Don't forget that first **-t** in **quantity**.*

EXERCISE 7.2 **In the space provided, write "correct" if the word is spelled correctly; if the word is misspelled, write its correct spelling in the space.**

1. mathematics _____

2. recognize _____

3. envirment _____

4. bachlor   _____

5. recommend   _____

6. grandmother   _____

7. choclate   _____

8. occasion   _____

9. canidate   _____

10. business   _____

11. exerise   _____

12. sophmore   _____

13. occurrence   _____

14. disipline   _____

15. granfather   _____

16. quantity   _____

17. sandwich   _____

18. dilemma   _____

19. congratulate   _____

20. puntuation   _____

SET C

word	syllables	notes
1. absen*c*e	2	Note that absence ends in *-ce*, NOT *-se*.
2. ac<u>comm</u>odate	4	Note the twin *c*'s and the twin *m*'s in **ac<u>comm</u>odate**.
3. am<u>on</u>g	2	Notice that there is NO *-u* in among.
4. cal<u>e</u>nd<u>a</u>r	3	Note the word **-lend-** in **calendar** and that the vowel in the last syllable is an *a* (-d*a*r).
5. co<u>mmitt</u>ee	3	Note the three double letters— *-mm, -tt, -ee*—in the spelling of **co<u>mmitt</u>ee**.
6. co<u>us</u>in	2	**Cousin** is another word in which careful pronunciation is of little spelling help. If **cousin** is a spelling demon of yours, consider using the approach outlined in the first part of this chapter.
7. def<u>i</u>n<u>ite</u>	3	As you can see, there is no *a* in **def<u>i</u>nite**.
8. el<u>ig</u>ible	4	**Eligible** is another word about which one must decide whether it should end in *-able* or *-ible*, and whether the "*l*" in the first syllable should be followed by *-a-,-e-,* or *-i-*. Unfortunately, there is no easy way to decide the preceding, so if **eligible** is a spelling demon of yours, use the strategy that works best for you in mastering such words.
9. emba<u>rr</u>ass	3	Don't ever be embarrassed by forgetting that there are two *r*'s in **emba<u>rr</u>ass**!
10. exp<u>la</u>nation	4	Note the word **plan** is contained in **exp<u>la</u>nation,** so don't spell this word "expl*ai*nation."
11. fami<u>liar</u>	3	Notice the word **liar** appears in **fami<u>liar</u>**.
12. <u>guara</u>ntee	3	Be sure to note the sequence of letters in this often misspelled word.
13. li<u>c</u>en<u>s</u>e	2	And be sure to get your *-c* and *-s* in **li<u>c</u>en<u>s</u>e** in the right order!

14. parallel   3

*It's easy to get mixed up spelling **parallel**, so you may need to invest extra time to master its spelling. You may—or you may not—find it helpful to remember the word starts with **para-**, followed by twin **l**'s and a final **-el**, or you may have found your own solution to spelling **parallel**.*

15. privilege   3

*Though it may sound as if the letters **-a** and **-d** should appear somewhere in **privilege**, neither letter does, so be sure you spell this challenging word correctly—not "privaledge," as some people are inclined to do—but you wouldn't be guilty of that, would you?*

16. restaurant   3

***Rest-** and **-rant** are two short words in **restaurant** that can help you spell this challenging word, so you just have to remember that **-au-** goes between these two short words.*

17. rhythm   2

*Most people find **rhythm** a difficult word to spell, and there is no foolproof method for mastering its spelling other than to (1) WRITE **rhythm** in large script on a piece of paper; (2) WRITE **rhythm** in the air with your eyes shut; (3) WRITE **rhythm** again on a piece of paer, and then check to make sure you spelled this word correctly.*

18. separate   3

*Remember the word **-par-** is in **separate** so you won't misspell it "seperate" as so many people do.*

19. tomorrow   3

*Remember that **tomorrow** is spelled with a double **-r**, NOT a double **-m**.*

20. vacuum   2

*Keep in mind that **vacuum** is spelled with one **-c** and -two **u**'s.*

EXERCISE 7.3 *In the space provided, write "correct" if the word is spelled correctly; if the word is misspelled, write its correct spelling.*

1. restaurent   _____

2. definate   _____

3. gaurantee   _____

4. amoung   _____

5. parallel   _____

6. rhytm   _____

7. vacuum   _____

8. absense   _____

9. tommorrow   _____

10. accommodate   _____

11. license   _____

12. seperate   _____

13. eligible   _____

14. cousin   _____

15. priviledge   _____

16. familiar   _____

17. explaination   _____

18. calendar   _____

19. embarass   _____

20. committee   _____

✓ CHECK-UP: Chapter 7, Spelling Challenges - 1

A *After reviewing this chapter, complete the following check-up by neatly circling the appropriate word.*

Veronica Pringleagogo

Casper Whipplesnade here, and once again I will relate to you the sad, and yes, the shocking true story of my attempt to date a lovely maiden of my community. As you no doubt recall, I had **(1)** (definately, definitely) resolved <u>not</u> to seek a date in the foreseeable future (I understand some of you have doubted my resolve. Why?) because I had no desire to eat humble pie as I had done on a number of prior **(2)** (occasions, ocassions). However, when I thought of some deserving girl whose life would be bolstered by my magnetic presence in her life, I surrendered my resolve (most reluctantly, you understand) to refrain from dating <u>IF</u> I could find a worthy young lady.

My search finally led to someone I thought might be a worthy **(3)** (canidate, candidate), someone who would grasp what a great **(4)** (privilege, priviledge) it would be to date me, the incomparable Casper Whipplesnade. The fortunate girl I selected for this great honor was none other than the captivating Veronica Pringleagogo.

Actually, I was not **(5)** (acquanted, acquainted) with Veronica until my **(6)** (cousin, couisen), Tootsie McKenzie, introduced me to Veronica this past winter after one of our school's basketball games. Veronica and Tootsie were **(7)** (among, amoung) our school's fifteen cheerleaders. Veronica dazzled me that evening with her cheerleading talent, which was demonstrated by her energetic dancing, leaps, backflips, and several high **(8)** (paralell, parallel) jumps with her partner from a towering pyramid formed by the other cheerleaders. I could readily see that Veronica was a **(9)** (valueble, valuable) member of the squad, but I feared that she was **(10)** (liable, lible) to **(11)** (accidently, accidentally) injure herself, thus never having the unspeakable pleasure of dating me. But thank goodness, all of her performances were flawless.

After the game, I strolled over to **(12)** (congradulate, congratulate) her on her impressive performances. Because her parents were waiting to take her home, we could not, much to my disappointment, and no doubt to hers, chitchat long, so we went our **(13)** (separate, seperate) ways.

However, to make a long story short, after I came to know Veronica much better during the next couple of weeks, I did indeed deem her worthy of going on a date with me, so I checked my cluttered **(14)** (calander, calendar), found a suitable day, and asked her for a date. In response to my question, Veronica replied, "What kind of date, Casper?"

I replied, "I've been thinking we could catch a movie Saturday afternoon, and then go to a **(15)** (restaurent, restaurant) for a bit of refreshment, such as a hamburger and a **(16)** (chocolate, choclate) sundae for dessert. Doesn't that sound like a fabulous date, Veronica?"

"It does sounds delightful, Casper, but to tell you the truth, I prefer to get some **(17)** (exercise, exerise) on Saturdays, so why don't we do something like play tennis, shoot baskets, or go skateboarding?" Veronica said. "What do you think about doing a couple of these activities, then jogging for four or five miles, Casper?"

My head and body were already revolting at the thought of doing even one of these tiring as well as boring exertions.

"Well, to tell you the truth, Veronica, I'm really not into such physical activities."

"Oh?" she exclaimed. "Okay, then," she continued, "how about some **(18)** (miniture, miniature) golf, badminton, archery, and bowling?" she asked.

I frowned and said, "Goodness, Veronica, you must like to sweat. I don't. I much prefer more intellectually challenging enterprises, such as tic-tac toe; charades; Red Rover, Red Rover; Billy Goat Gruff; or playing cards like Old Maid and Uncle Wiggily. Perhaps we could top off our time together by playing some music, that is, if you have any talent along those lines."

"Oh, Casper, do you play an instrument?"

I sweetly, then humbly replied, "Actually, Veronica, I play two instruments exceedingly well."

"How wonderful, Casper. What two instruments do you play? I confess that I am limited to playing just one—the piano."

I attempted to soothe her discomfort by saying, "Don't be **(19)** (embarassed, embarrassed), Veronica. Not everyone is, or can be, an accomplished musician as I have the distinction of being. In fact, I'm **(20)** (practilly, practically) a pro."

"Wow, Casper! I'm so honored that you are spending time with me! Musicians such as you have to possess such extraordinary **(21)** (discipline, dissipline) to **(22)** (suceed, succeed) on such a lofty level," Veronica gushed, though I detected a hint of insincerity and, yes, even skepticism in her voice.

But I said, "That's so true, Veronica; yet most **(23)** (amatuers, amateurs) such as yourself don't understand that." I continued, "Well, let's turn our attention to you. So you play the piano—what piano book are you currently playing from? Clara Bartowski's *Book One?*"

"Oh, no, Casper. I finished that book when I was in third grade. In fact, now I only play from the most advanced piano books my teacher provides me. To tell you the truth, Casper, I can play from most any piano book, regardless of how advanced it is or the type of music it contains."

"Oh, really?" I skeptically remarked, surprised that Veronica had such an overblown ego, something I can't abide in anyone. At this point, my feelings of affection for Veronica started slipping away. Frankly, I have never been able to **(24)** (accommodate, accomodate) my feelings for people who think too highly of themselves; I do, in fact, resent such egotistical creatures. (Why, I wondered, can't people be more like I am—humble, dignified, and modest despite possessing an array of impressive talents?)

"So, Veronica, what piece of so-called 'challenging' music are you currently playing?"

"Well, Casper, I'm striving to memorize Chopin's beautiful *Fantasy Impromptu.* Such a captivating classical composition!"

I wasn't impressed. I said, "I've never heard of that Shoppin' person, and the title of that piece certainly doesn't sound very challenging. Do you play any other kind of music besides the boring classical type, Veronica?"

"Oh, yes! I find great pleasure in playing rock and roll, country, popular, folk, and **(25)** (rythm, rhythm) and blues. I'm also the piano accompanist for our school's jazz and dance bands; didn't you know that?" I ignored that question because I *didn't* know she was for the simple reason I don't pay attention as to who's playing in the school band.

Veronica continued her ramblings, "By the way, Casper, we got sidetracked before you could answer my question as to what two instruments you play, and I would also appreciate knowing your favorite genre of music."

("Genre, what's that?" I muttered to myself. It sounds like some skin disease, or perhaps Veronica stutters from time to time.) I replied, "Veronica, please don't think me immodest, because although I am an outstanding musician—**(26)** (amoung, among) my many talents—I am truly a down-to-earth person. But in answer to your inquiry, I started playing my radio and cd appliances at an early age, and at that time I **(27)** (aquired, acquired) a taste for all types of music. You might say I was a child prodigy. **(28)** (Incidently, Incidentally), I should **(29)** (probably, probly) also mention that I am widely **(30)** (recognized, recconized) in many circles for my ability to use my smartphone to locate any type of music that one might desire."

Veronica was apparently so awestruck by what I had just said because all should could do was stare at me in a shocked condition for the longest time before saying, "You're putting me on, Casper Whipplesnade, and I don't like it one bit! You obviously don't appreciate my musical ability (true), and you apparently have none! So go away from me immediately and don't ever try to talk to me again!"

What a nasty **(31)** (temperment, temperament) that young lady possesses. Good riddance!

What was I to think about this sudden change in Veronica's behavior? Such an **(32)** (occurence, occurrence) could only lead me to conclude that she had joined the long line of my contemporaries who are jealous of me. In this instance, I had true musical ability, whereas she had obviously exaggerated her piano playing ability, even to the point that she stated that she played in our school's jazz band, though I had never witnessed her doing so. However, since

Veronica and I had our little "pleasant" talk, I have made some inquiries and found out that—brace yourself—she was, surprisingly, telling the truth about everything—but so what? Her piano ability, I am convinced, is no match for her **(33)** (absense, absence) of any humility. So this brings me to the point of wondering this: Why can't Veronica be more like me—blessed with impressive talent but always modest, dignified, and down-to-earth?

B *Neatly circle the correctly spelled word in each of the following sentences.*

1. Is your sidewalk (paralell, parallel) to the street?

2. Our daughter plans on getting her driver's (license, lisence) this summer.

3. She will be (eligable, eligible) to try when she turns sixteen in August.

4. What (explaination, explanation) did Ted give you for not showing up for work?

5. I (guarantee, garantee) you Ted will have an interesting excuse.

6. Loren, will you please (vacume, vacuum) the rug in the hallway?

7. Margaret is serving on the nominating (comittee, committee).

8. (Tommorrow, Tomorrow) we're driving to Wichita to see our (granfather, grandfather) and (granmother, grandmother).

9. A cheeseburger with grilled onions is still my favorite (sandwich, sanwich).

10. To my utter surprise, Rusty the Plunger said he's not (familar, familiar) with this type of plumbing problem, that is, a leaking faucet.

11. I don't think my friend Juan is going to be a (bachlor, bachelor) much longer since he seems to be deeply in love with Ginny.

12. I'm a (sophmore, sophomore) at the state university, and (mathematics, mathamatics) is my major.

13. Kate, please check my (puntuation, punctuation) in my job application letter.

14. Yes, I'm in a (dilemma, delimma), but you seem to be in a (quandry, quandary) as well.

15. Where is the southernmost (boundry, boundary) of your property, Mike?

16. Canada's (Parliment, Parliament) is now in session.

17. Mortimer was in show (bisness, business) for years.

18. We had only one (occurance, occurrence) of a customer complaining about our service this past hour.

19. The newspaper expressed (critism, criticism) for the government's relaxation of numerous regulations having to do with the (environment, enviroment).

20. The sheer (quantity, quanity) of Bruce's baseball cards is unbelievable.

21. Wendy speaks in a delightful English (dilect, dialect).

22. I think Rory will (probably, probly) return to college after he climbs a few more challenging mountains.

23. Did Melissa (aquire, acquire) her tan from the sun, a salon, or a bottle?

24. (Coincidently, Coincidentally,) Reefer's oldest brother Rafer was also captain of the soccer team when he was a senior in high school.

25. The jury's verdict of (acquittal, aquittal) stunned those in the courtroom.

26. According to the TV meteorologist, the powerful and frigid wind we're experiencing originated in the (artic, arctic) zone.

27. The physical therapist (basically, basicaly) told Manny he'd have to be more faithful in doing the (exerise, exercise) program assigned to him if he truly wanted to become stronger.

28. The beautician (reccomended, recommended) to her patron that she shorten her hair by several inches.

29. This bus can (accommodate, accomodate) only thirty passengers.

30. The band instructor told the young drummer that she was responsible for establishing and maintaining the (rythm, rhythm) for whatever type of music was being played.

Spelling Challenges – 2

The places where spelling errors are most frequently made in the following words are once again underlined, and the number of syllables in each word is provided to help in its pronunciation, which, as has been previously mentioned, can often contribute to a word's correct spelling. Spelling suggestions are again provided.

SET A

	word	syllables	notes
1.	accept<u>able</u>	4	*Though **-able** and **-ible** sound the same, **acceptable** ends in **-able**—not -ible.*
2.	ach<u>ie</u>ve	2	*As you can see, **achieve** follows the rule of "**i** before **e** …"*
3.	advis<u>able</u>	4	***Advisable** is another word that ends in **-able**— not -ible.*
4.	a<u>pp</u>a<u>rent</u>	3	*Notice the double **pp**, and let the word **-rent** help you spell **apparent**.*
5.	arg<u>u</u>ment	3	*The letter **-e**, which appears in **argue**, is dropped when **argument** is spelled.*
6.	at<u>hl</u>etic	3	*Spelling or pronounncing **athletic** in four syllables, as in "athaletic" is a major boo-boo, particularly if you consider yourself an **athlete**.*
7.	bel<u>ie</u>ve	3	*The rule "**i** before **e**" applies to **believe**, doesn't it?*

8. canc<u>e</u>led   2   *Though this word is often spelled with a double -l (cancelled), the proper spelling is usually considered* **canceled**.

9. Cari<u>bb</u>ean   4   *As you can see, there is <u>one</u> -r and <u>two</u> -b's (**bb**) in **Caribbean**; perhaps remembering that -rib- + -bean go together in **Ca<u>rib</u>bean** will help.*

10. cat<u>e</u>gory   4   *Though **cat<u>e</u>gory**'s second syllable sounds like an -a when it is pronounced, it is actually an -e that represents the sound—which may not make sense, but that's the way it is!*

11. chang<u>e</u>able   3   *The -e is kept for pronunciation purposes:* **chang<u>e</u>able**, *not changable.*

12. collect<u>ible</u>   4   *Finally, we have a word that ends in -**ible**:* **collect<u>ible</u>**, *not collect<u>a</u>ble.*

13. coll<u>e</u>ge   2   *For goodness' sake, don't misspell* **coll<u>e</u>ge** *as "collage."*

14. diff<u>e</u>rence   3   *If we misspell* **diff<u>e</u>rence**, *it may be due to the way we pronounce it: "diffrance," which is probably okay when we <u>say</u> this word but not when we <u>write</u> it!*

15. drunk<u>e</u>n<u>n</u>ess   3   *It's easy to omit the second -**n** in spelling* **drunk<u>e</u>n<u>n</u>ess**— *but don't!*

16. dum<u>b</u>bell   2   *Dum**b**bell is a compound word (**dumb** + **bell**) and although the -**b** in **dumb** is not pronounced, it should be included when this word is spelled.*

17. experi<u>e</u>nce   4   *Note that* **experi<u>e</u>nce** *is spelled with an -**e** after the **i**.*

18. Feb<u>r</u>uary   4   *We might gloss over the -**r** in* **Feb<u>r</u>uary** *when we <u>say</u> this month, but the -**r** needs to be included when we <u>spell</u> it.*

19. for<u>ei</u>gn   2   **For<u>ei</u>gn** *is an exception to the rule "**i** before **e**," as you can see.*

20. fr<u>ie</u>nd   1   *The word* **fr<u>ie</u>nd** *returns us to the rule mentioned in #19, doesn't it?*

21. ga<u>u</u>ge   1   *Pronouncing **gauge** aloud doesn't help when it's being spelled as the **-a** and **-u** are regularly misplaced, so that **gauge** is spelled "<u>guage</u>"; but you don't make this mistake, right?*

EXERCISE 8.1   *In the space provided, write "correct" if the word is spelled correctly; otherwise, indicate its correct spelling.*

1. Carribean _____

2. drunkeness _____

3. athletic _____

4. Febuary _____

5. advisable _____

6. collage _____

7. apparant _____

8. foriegn _____

9. catagory _____

10. achieve _____

11. differance _____

12. guage _____

13. changeable _____

14. acceptable _____

15. freind   _____

16. arguement   _____

17. experience   _____

18. beleive   _____

19. collectable   _____

20. canceled   _____

SET B

	word	syllables	notes
1.	gui**dance**	2	Notice the word **-dance** appears in **guidance**.
2.	h**ei**ght	1	Remembering **-eight** will ensure you spell **height** correctly.
3.	h**y**g**ie**ne	2	As you can see, the **-i** sound in the first syllable of **hygiene** is represented by **-y**, and the **i** before **e** rule applies in the second syllable.
4.	independ**e**nt	4	When **independent** is misspelled, it's often due to an **-a** in the last syllable instead of the correct **-e**.
5.	ignor**a**nce	3	**Ignorance** presents that common challenge of whether **-a** or **-e** is the correct choice to use.
6.	intellig**e**nce	4	Oh happy day! This time **-e** is the correct choice.
7.	jewel**ry**	2	Pronunciation can help us spell this word correctly as it's **jewelry** (**jewel-ry**), not "jew-lery."
8.	j**u**d**g**ment	2	What letter would many people expect after **judg-** but isn't there?
9.	l**ei**sure	2	**Leisure** is another of those pesky "Is it **ei** or **ie**?" words.

10. liaison   3   Yep, **liaison** is spelled the way it appears here. A common mistake is to omit the second -*i*.

11. maintenance   3   **Maintenance** has -**ten** stuck in the middle—and it's pronounced and spelled **main-ten-ance**, not main-tain—ence.

12. mischievous   3   Many people, including me, find **mischievous** a challenging word to spell because (1) there is the *i* before *e* order to consider, and (2) at least in my case, a tendency to insert an *i* in the last syllable -**vious**, which, of course, results in a misspelling.

13. mediocre   4   **Mediocre** is challenging because we pronounce it "mediokur" but the last syllable is spelled -**cre**, so pronunciation is of limited help.

14. neighbor   2   You recall, don't you, that it's "*i* before *e* <u>except</u> after *c* or when sounded like *a* as in **neighbor** and **weigh**"?

15. noticeable   4   The -*e* in **notice** is kept when spelling **noticeable**, and the word ends in -**able**, not -*ible*.

16. omission   3   Keep in mind that there is a "**mission**" in **omission**!

17. original   4   Well now, you probably know how to pronounce this word [uh-RIG-uh-nil), but like so many words in the English language, knowing how a word is pronounced doesn't always help in its spelling, does it? **Original** is such a word for many people. If this word is a spelling demon of yours, focusing on the vowels should help.

18. patriotic   4   When **patriotic** is misspelled, it's usually because the -*r* and -*i* are reversed.

19. poison   2   It is tempting to use -*e* when spelling this word, but nope, it doesn't have one: **poison**.

20. pro<u>nun</u>ciation   5   *We've been kicking this word around a lot in this book, so we should be sure we know how to spell it.* **Pronunciation** *is often misspelled pronounciation, but there is no* **-o** *after the* **-n** *in the second syllable.*

EXERCISE 8.2   **If the word is spelled correctly, write "correct" in the space provided; otherwise, indicate its correct spelling in the space provided.**

1. mediocre   _____

2. independant   _____

3. original   _____

4. liesure   _____

5. poisen   _____

6. judgment   _____

7. intellegence   _____

8. noticable   _____

9. hieght   _____

10. maintainance   _____

11. guidence   _____

12. pronunciation   _____

13. hygiene   _____

14. omission   _____

15. jewelery _____

16. patriotic _____

17. ignorence _____

18. neighbor _____

19. liason _____

20. mischevious _____

SET C

1-15 in this set are concerned with a number of commonly misspelled words, often due to the fact that they contain silent letters that are easily (and logically) omitted, so pronunciation, which is helpful in spelling so many words, is of limited assistance when it comes to spelling these words. (The silent letters are in boldface and underlined.) There are, of course, many other words containing silent letters (de**b**t, i**s**land, **k**nee, **k**nock, thum**b**, **w**reck, **w**rite, et. al.), but the following are among the prominent ones deserving your special attention. The number of syllables in each word is again included; trusting this information may help you master its pronunciation and, in turn, its spelling. Additional spelling suggestions are also included for a few of the words.

word	syllables	notes
1. adolescent	4	
2. benign	2	
3. column	2	
4. fascinate	3	
5. ghastly	2	
6. knowledge	2	

7. m̲nemonic   3   *Mnemonic is a memory strategy in which the first letter of each item to be remembered is used to form a "trigger" word, as in this example: The "trigger" word H̲O̲M̲E̲S̲ helps us recall the Great Lakes of H̲uron, O̲ntario, M̲ichigan, E̲rie, and S̲uperior.*

8. plum̲b̲er   2
9. promp̲t   1
10. questionn̲aire   3   *Many (most?) people spell questionnaire with one -n, but not you, right?*

11. sc̲issors   2
12. solem̲n   2
13. straigh̲t   1
14. sub̲tle   2
15. Wed̲nesday   2

Numbers **16-21** are concerned with words that drop an **-e** when their derivatives are formed.

16. disaster   →   disastrous

17. enter   →   entrance

18. hinder   →   hindrance

19. hunger   →   hungry

20. monster   →   monstrous

21. remember →   remembrance

You may have observed from an earlier chapter that when adding a consonant suffix to most words ending in *-e*, the *-e* is usually kept (see also examples above, p. 35):

manage → management

complete → completely

advance → advancement

However, as has been pointed out in a few cases above, the *-e* is sometimes dropped:

22. acknowledge → acknowledgment

23. argue → argument

24. judge → judgment

25. nine → ninth

26. true → truly

EXERCISE 8.3 *Neatly circle the correctly spelled word.*

1. fascinate   fasinate

2. hunger   hungar

3. gastly   ghastly

4. monsterous   monstrous

5. questionnaire   questionaire

6. sissors — scissors
7. plummar — plumber
8. ninth — nineth
9. enterance — entrance
10. adolescent — adolesent
11. rememberance — remembrance
12. judgment — judgement
13. argument — arguement
14. knowlege — knowledge
15. acknowlegement — acknowledgment
16. truely — truly
17. subtle — suttle
18. disasterous — disastrous
19. benine — benign
20. prompt — promt
21. column — colum
22. memonics — mnemonics
23. straite — straight
24. Wenesday — Wednesday
25. solemn — solem
26. hinderance — hindrance

✓ CHECK-UP: Chapter 8, Spelling Challenges – 2

A *After reviewing this chapter, complete the following check-up that follows by neatly circling the appropriate word.*

Edith Esterhelmsly

Yes, you lucky readers, it's "the often imitated but never equaled" Casper Whipplesnade taking time to write to you poor souls once again, so fasten your seat belts as I tell you another exciting episode of my search for an attractive and intelligent girl who would appreciate what an honor it would be to make my acquaintance and, if she met my high standards, to be my special friend.

As I've related to you previously, I thought on a few occasions that I had found such a worthy girl, but, alas, that belief proved to be painfully wrong, though I have no doubt that each girl rues the day she passed over her chance to be my girlfriend, so they now must feel **(1)** (ghastly, gastly). But let's not dwell on the **(2)** (disasterous, disastrous) past.

Instead, let me tell you about Edith Esterhelmsly. [The **(3)** (pronunciation, pronounciation) of her last name, though lengthy, is easy, isn't it?] Edith's **(4)** (intelligence, intelligance) was readily **(5)** (apparent, apparant) from the moment we had our first fairly lengthy conversation. I quickly **(6)** (believed, beleived) that by my wise **(7)** (guidance, guidence), Edith would indeed become a **(8)** (truely, truly) remarkable young lady.

Edith is in the same grade in school as I am, so there's no significant **(9)** (differance, difference) in our age, though this is not true of our **(10)** (hieghts, heights) as she is at least five inches taller than I am, but that happenstance certainly isn't any type of **(11)** (hindrance, hinderance) to what eventually developed into a **(12)** (fasinating, fascinating) relationship which, as I can attest, is not true of most **(13)** (adolesent, adolescent) romances.

My first recollections of dear Edith was observing her working at her folks' convenience store (there is a sign in the store's front window that states, *"If we don't have it, you don't need it."*) Other than saying an occasional "hello" to each other at the store, which I didn't frequent too often because it's a couple of miles or so from where I live, Edith and I had never conversed to any great length, which in retrospect, must have greatly disappointed her.

However, after she and I had been selected to read to students attending the elementary school located across the expanse of lawn from our middle school, Edith's **(14)** (sutle, subtle) and sometimes **(15)** (mischievous, mischeivious) ways became attractive to me. Edith and I would talk and laugh as we walked between the two schools. We never had even a small **(16)** (arguement, argument). Soon we also managed to meet at other times during and after school, and not surprisingly, we became inseparable. We would traipse hand in hand over to the elementary school at 1:00 p.m. Monday through Friday where Edith would read books to a second grade class, and I would read to a third grade class for half an hour. I read them stories from an **(17)** (original, orginal) Uncle Wiggily book—now a much-sought-after **(18)** (collectable, collectible). My dear third graders soon loved Uncle Wiggily and, in my flawless **(19)** (judgment, judgement), they were soon captivated by me as well as this old rabbit gentleman's many adventures.

It was an honor to be chosen as a reader, and I was pleased when I was asked to be one. I must admit, however, that I was surprised that I had not been chosen some time before, especially because Bozo Rademaker, a loser who is fast becoming an irritation to me, had been a reader the previous semester, and Bozo couldn't possibly compare to me as either a reader or as a role model for these darling young students, many of whom probably idolized me, and rightly so.

Okay, so what if Bozo was more **(20)** (atheletic, athletic) than I am? I certainly don't want to get all hot and sweaty running around a field, track, or court—it's obviously difficult to possess good **(21)** (hygiene, hygeine) when you're contending with lots of sweat. Furthermore, despite the fact that Bozo somehow manages to get on the high honor roll every semester, his **(22)** (ignorence, ignorance) about how to interact effectively with others was obvious to me. I am also convinced that Bozo has an unbelievable ego, something I, who's always been humble, cannot abide; and his overall **(23)** (knowledge, knowlege) of human nature was lacking. Indeed, I think it's his inflated ego that will eventually lead to his downfall. Poor Bozo. He should try to be more like I am—intelligent, talented, dignified, yet always humble.

But be that as it may, reading to the third readers was the highlight of my school day, especially after Edith and I began holding hands as we walked between the two schools. When in the company of Edith, I finally had **(24)** (achieved, acheived) the bliss I had been searching for!

It's not surprising, then, that Edith and I became inseparable. We walked to school together, and we met every chance we had at school. On Saturdays, Edith usually worked at her parents' convenience store doing much of the **(25)** (maintainance, maintenance) work, including dusting the shelves and sweeping the floor. She also saw to it that each **(26)** (column, colum) of goods on every shelf was **(27)** (straight, strait).

When we weren't together, we texted each other, both night and day. Our close relationship was **(28)** (noticable, noticeable), especially by my mother, who remarked one evening, "Aren't you and Edith devoting a bit too much time to each other, Casper?"

"Well, Mother dear," I patiently explained, "Edith is special, and she adores me, Mom, as most girls, both young and old generally do once they have the privilege of making my acquaintance."

"There you go again, Casper, letting your ego get the better of you," Mom retorted. Dear old Mom. She had evidently forgotten what young love is like, and what a remarkable son she has in me.

However, I didn't respond to Mom's remark in a harsh, defensive manner; instead, I went upstairs to my room and read six text messages I had received during the last half hour, all from my sweet, dear Edith. The last text from her came five minutes after her previous one, clearly indicating her despair from having to endure going nearly half an hour without hearing from me. It read, "Casper darling, why haven't I heard from you in the last thirty minutes? Have you fallen out of love with me? Have you suddenly taken ill, been kidnapped, or what? Please respond ASAP! Frantically, your adoring Edith."

Our relationship survived, continuing for several more weeks, even when Edith became even more possessive. Frankly, by this time I must confess that my mother may have been right in saying that Edith and our relationship was "a bit too much." Edith was a wonderful girl all right, but all of the attention she devoted to me night and day made me feel as if I were being smothered.

Sensitive girl that she was, Edith detected that my ardor to be with her every possible minute had cooled considerably, particularly since I had avoided her at school, including our daily walk to school, and because I **(29)** (canceled, cancelled) a movie date with her.

One morning before school, Edith said, in a most **(30)** (solemn, solem) voice, "Casper, darling, I can tell that you are tiring of me. Why? Are we spending too much time with each other?"

"Absolutely. I mean no. Yes. No. Yes. No. Yes," I stammered.

"Edith, my peach," I continued, your influence these past two months has made me an even more noble person than I was before, so along with my handsomeness, talents, intelligence, and modesty, I am indebted to you, but I think the time has come to break off our close relationship and just be friends."

As I was saying these heartbreaking words to her, Edith had a look on her face as if I had given her **(31)** (poisen, poison). She scurried away without a word, no doubt because she was about to weep over losing me, poor, poor heartbroken Edith.

So I was surprised, but not necessarily disappointed, that she didn't text me that evening, but I was even more surprised—actually shocked—at school the next morning when Edith and Bozo Rademaker (of all people!) were strolling hand in hand, passing me near the **(32)** (enterance, entrance) of the school without acknowledging me, with not even so much as a glance or a nod.

I concluded, after I recovered from the shock, that Edith was a **(33)** (changable, changeable) young lady who, though providing me with a pleasant interlude, would now, despite her painful loss of me as her boyfriend, rush into the arms of anyone, including such losers as Bozo Rademaker.

So I vowed once again (a vow that I would keep this time, I vowed! *[Are you following me here?]*). Yes, in fact, I would ban all contact with girls and devote what little **(34)** (leisure, liesure) time I had to improving my stamp collection, something that was impossible to do when I was constantly hounded by the faithless, ungrateful Edith Esterhelmsly. "Yes," I muttered to myself, " a girl would be fortunate if I even spoke to her, not only now but also in the future, and maybe even through **(35)** (collage, college)."

Then, as if by magic, my **(36)** my (remembrance, rememberance) of Vera Von Failingstock suddenly appeared in my remarkable brain. (For your information, Vera was a girl I met some months ago when we both were dog walkers for various

(37) (neighbors, nieghbors). Hmm, perhaps I should get in touch with the lovely Vera.

Ah, but no. I have vowed once more not to get involved in any more romantic entanglements. Yet … (*Hasn't poor, egotistical Casper gone through this dilemma of-his-own-making a number of times before?*)

B **If all four words in a set are spelled correctly, write "Correct" on the provided line. Otherwise, circle any misspelled words (there might be more than one per set) and indicate the correct spelling for each.**

1. gauge patriotic Wednesday acheive _____

2. Carribbean drunkeness prompt independent _____

3. omission questionnaire scissors jewelry _____

4. judgment experience solemn hungry _____

5. medicre benign laison dumbell _____

6. mnemonics category adviseable foreign _____

7. collectable friend Febuary plumber _____

Academic Words

The spelling words in this chapter include those related to a variety of academic subjects; many of these words you may already know how to spell, while others may be a spelling challenge for you.

These words are certainly not the only academic terms you should know (or will learn) how to spell, but mastery of them will help to provide you with a solid academic spelling foundation on which to build. Each word's phonetic pronunciation is included as well as a line space under the presentation of the word so that you can practice writing the correct spelling of the word at least twice.

For those words you may find especially difficult to spell, consider using the *Three-W Steps Method* that has been described on page viii, or use any method that you have personally found helpful.

Some of these words have appeared in previous chapters but because of their frequent use in academia, they are repeated here. In some instances, certain terms are defined as they may not be as well-known to you as the other words are.

SET A

1. academy (ah KAD duh me)
    academia (ak uh DEM e me ah)
    academic (ak uh DEM ik)

_____

_____

_____

2. aesthetics (es THET iks)
   <u>Aesthetics</u> is concerned with the study of beauty, particularly beauty associated with painting, sculpture, architecture and music.

   _____

3. adviser or advisor (ad VIS ur)

   _____

4. apparatus (ap puh RAT us)

   _____

5. athletics (ath LET iks)

   _____

6. author (AU thor)

   _____

7. avant-garde (ah vant GARD)
   <u>Avant-garde</u> is a French term referring to an advanced or experimental type of art.

   _____

8. behavior (be HAV ior)

   _____

9. calligraphy (kuh LEG ruh fe)
   <u>Calligraphy</u> is the art of beautiful handwriting.

   _____

10. caricature (KAR uh kuh chur)
    A caricature is a cartoon representation of a person or an object exaggerated in some manner for the purpose of humor or ridicule.

    _____

11. catalyst (KAT ah list)
    A catalyst is (1) a substance that speeds up a chemical reaction; (2) any agent that speeds up a specific action.

    _____

12. commencement (kuh MENS ment)
    Commencement is associated with high school and college graduations. The word commencement, however, means the beginning or start of something.

    _____

13. curriculum (kur RIK yu lum)
    Curriculum refers to the courses of study offered by a school or college.

    _____

14. deduction (de DUK shun) and (15) induction (in DUK shun)
    Deduction is reasoning that starts with an accepted principle and leads to specific instances that support the accepted principle.

    Induction, on the other hand, is the reaching of a conclusion after gathering supporting information.

    _____

    _____

16. democracy (de MOK ra see)

_____

17. diagnosis (di ag NO sus)

_____

18. dormant (DOR munt)
    <u>Dormant</u> describes an organism that is inactive and not developing.

_____

19. dormitory (DOR muh tor re)

_____

20. environment (en VI ron ment)

_____

21. experiment (ex PER uh ment)

_____

22. hyperbole (hy PER bo le)
    <u>Hyperbole</u> is an obvious, intentional exaggeration not meant to be taken literally.

_____

23. premise (PRE mis)
    A <u>premise</u> is an assumption upon which an action or conclusion is based.

_____

EXERCISE 9.1 *Before doing this exercise, be sure you are familiar with both the spelling and meaning of every word in Set A; then in the space, write the word suggested by the context of the sentence.*

1. This word contains "iron." _____.

2. Reasoning that involves gathering facts before reaching a conclusion is known as_____ reasoning.

3. A person who has written a book, poem or other type of writing is, of course, referred to as the _____ of those writings.

4. An agent that speeds up a chemical reaction is called a(an) _____.

5. I was told to make an appointment with my college _____ if I wanted to add or drop a course.

6. I had to explain to my little brother that Lebron James didn't actually score 1000 points last night; that was just _____.

7. The wedding invitations were hand-printed with beautiful _____.

8. My college psychology course is concerned with both normal and abnormal _____.

9. A number of artists in the nineteenth century were _____ as they pioneered a new style of painting.

10. Though the college I attend is small, its _____ is broad, offering courses ranging from accounting to zoology.

11. The researchers started with the assumption that the newly developed medicine would prove effective for diabetes, but after examining patients two months later they realized their initial _____ was not supported by the evidence.

12. A _____ of the governor appeared in this morning's paper, and the cartoon exaggerated the size of his ears and nose.

13. A (an) _____ of some kind, with a large microscope and a couple of lights as well as other gizmos attached to it, was sitting on the lab table assigned to my partner and me.

14. It wasn't such a brilliant _____ to conclude the book must be Samantha's; her name was written inside the front cover!

15. I've always loved _____ of all kinds, including soccer, basketball, and ring-around-the-rosy.

16. Surprise! Surprise! The science _____ I did in front of the class actually worked!

17. The teacher showed numerous pictures of famous paintings and sculptures in an effort to stimulate his students' _____ sensibilities.

18. Instead of being called a "high school," the secondary school Barb attended in New England was called a(n) _____.

19. If a country is a(an) _____, then the ultimate power of the government rests in the hands of its citizens.

20. Unlike bears, squirrels are active, not_____, during the winter months.

21. Rex moved into a new campus _____this fall.

22. Is my ankle broken or only sprained, Dr. Bones? What's your _____?

23. The _____ of the game followed shortly after the child exclaimed over the loudspeaker, "Play ball!"

SET B

1. analyze (AN ah lies)

_____

2. atrophy (AT rah fee)
   <u>Atrophy</u> refers to the wasting away of muscles due to illness, injury, or inactivity.

_____

3. benign (bah NINE) and (4) malignant (muh LIG nunt)
   Something that is <u>benign</u> is harmless; something that is <u>malignant</u> is threatening to life and often deadly.

_____

_____

5. bibliography (bib le OG rah fee)
   A <u>bibliography</u> is a list of books and other sources used in writing a research report or other document.

_____

6. carpe diem (KAR pah DE em)
   <u>Carpe diem</u> is a Latin phrase that means "seize the day" or "enjoy the present."

_____

7. cognitive (KOG nuh tiv)
   <u>Cognitive</u> refers to the mental processes involved in thinking and understanding.

_____

8. connotation (KON ah TA shun), and (9) denotation (DE no TA shun)
<u>Connotation</u> is a word's suggested meaning, such as the word "fall" which many people associate with football, colored leaves, and crisp temperatures.

<u>Denotation</u> is a word's exact meaning, such as "fall" being the season of the year that embraces the months of September, October, and November.

_____

_____

10. edema (ah DEM muh)
<u>Edema</u> is a swelling caused by a surplus of fluids.

_____

11. empirical (em PIR ah kal)
<u>Empirical</u> refers to evidence that has been actually experienced or observed.

_____

12. etymology (ET uh mol luh je)
<u>Etymology</u> is the study of the origins of words and how their meanings and usages may have changed through the years.

_____

13. figurative (FIG yur ah tiv) and (14) literal (LIT uh rul) languages
<u>Figurative</u> language is the use of imaginative, colorful, or exaggerated words to express one's opinions, ideas, or descriptions, such as *Aiden can hit a baseball a mile or more.*

<u>Literal</u> language, on the other hand, is limiting one's words to their strict meanings, such as *Aiden can hit a baseball over 300 feet.*

_____

15. genre (ZHAN ra)

Genre is a category of literature, such as a novel, biography, autobiography, short story, mystery, or poetry.

16. hierarchy (HI ark kee)

Hierarchy generally refers to a ranking of people based on ability, social status, or professional standing. Here's an example: *When I worked as a busboy at Sloppy Joe's, I quickly learned that I was at the bottom of the restaurant's hierarchy and that the chef was at the top of it.*

17. hypothesis (hi POTH uh sus)

Hypothesis is a logical explanation that requires a thorough investigation before it can be said to be true.

18. inherent (in HAIR ant)

Inherent refers to a trait that is considered inborn. Example: *Martin's artistic ability appears to be inherent as he was drawing impressive pictures when he was just three years old.*

19. laboratory (LAB ruh TOR ee)

Notice that *labor* is involved in the spelling of laboratory.

20. plagiarism (PLAY juh riz um)
    <u>Plagiarism</u> is the copying of words or ideas of another writer or speaker and then presenting them as one's original work.

EXERCISE 9.2 *Before doing this exercise, be sure you are familiar with both the spelling and meaning of every word in Set B; then in the space write the word suggested by the context of the sentence.*

1. This rather long word contains a synonym for "work." _____

2. Rita apparently possesses_____ musical ability as she's been singing like an angel since she was two years old.

3. The _____ of an orchestra conductor that always comes to my mind is of an old gent with long unruly grey hair who's tossing his head hither and yon while his tuxedo flaps all around as he makes countless gyrations with his wildly swinging arms. How about you? What pictures or associations come to *your* mind when you think of an orchestra director?

4. On the other hand, the_____, or strict definition of an orchestra director, is a person who guides a group of musicians, often from a rostrum, and who indicates from his or her gestures how a piece of music is to be played, such as loudly, softly, slowly, or rapidly.

5. For most card games, the ranking, or_____, of the cards is (from lowest to highest) deuce of clubs to ace of spades.

6. In the writing of your research paper, you can avoid _____ by listing all the sources, such as books, periodicals, and newspapers, you used in your research.

7. The _____ appears at the end of your paper. In addition, be sure to insert quotation marks around the exact words of any person you include in your statements.

8. _____ is an expression meaning "Seize the Day." The origin, or 9. _____, of this expression can be traced to the Latin language.

10. It will take several days to _____ all the data we have gathered, so at this point, I don't know what our explanation will be for the unusual winter weather we have been experiencing this season.

11. I believe our theory, or _____, is correct, but we can't accept or reject it presently because, as is true of any theory, research must be completed and thoroughly analyzed before any conclusions are drawn.

12. In other words, we will need _____ evidence, that is, evidence that is verifiable or observable, before it can be said that our theory is likely correct.

13. Lorenzo, unless you start working out again, including lifting weights, your impressive muscles will no doubt _____.

14. One of Marge's elbows is swollen because it was hit by a softball; however, the doctor said the swelling, which he referred to as_____, would subside in a few days.

15. According to this source, a child's _____ abilities, or mental skills, are well-developed by the time he or she is three.

16. Although my dad enjoys mystery films, his favorite movie _____ is western, particularly when starring Roy Rogers and his horse Trigger.

17. My motorscooter's top speed is forty mph, and that is the _____ truth.

18. Obviously, my girlfriend was using_____ language when she said the scooter could reach a top speed of 100 mph; that's a colorful description, but it's also an obvious exaggeration!

19. Our dog Fido might appear to be nasty, even a _____ canine capable of taking a person's life, but I assure you he actually possesses a 20. _____ disposition; why good old Fido is so sweet that he wouldn't bite a mail carrier.

 **CHECK-UP: Chapter 9, Academic Words**

A **Circle the correctly spelled word.**

Vera Venuslike

Hello devoted fans! Yes indeed, this is the one and only Casper Whipplesnade, your hero, here to share with you, my faithful followers, my latest thrilling romantic adventure. (You *are* keeping track of them, aren't you?) Of course, you'll no doubt also recall that I once again had earnestly vowed not to date for a long time, based upon my unbelievable (what's wrong with these girls?) and disappointing outcomes with those of the female persuasion during the past several months. My **(1)** (dediction, deduction) was that the **(2)** (enviorment, environment) for dating would undoubtedly improve as the school year progressed. Meanwhile, my dating ambitions would remain **(3)** (dormant, dorment).

But then I met the lovely Vera, a girl I had become acquainted with last spring when we were both dog walkers. (By the way, my **(4)** (hypothesis, hypothisis) is that there is no better way to meet a girl than by walking a dog.) I had not seen Vera since then as she attends a different middle school than I do. I can't imagine in retrospect why I didn't attempt to date Vera back then as she no doubt would have been eternally grateful to me if I had, but there is no accounting for one's **(5)** (behavor, behavior) at times. Probably my mind was still befuddled by Twallah's shocking betrayal of me at the time I met Vera. I was convinced now, however, that the **(6)** (commensment, commencement) of a beautiful relationship between Vera Venuslike and me was about to begin. I said to myself, "Casper, you wonderful person, **(7)** ("carpe diem, carp dieum"), or to you who are not on my lofty intellectual level, "*Seize the day!*"

So early one Saturday morning, I scurried over to a location I knew was on Vera's dog walking route. I had assumed she was still engaged in that activity, and my assumption proved to be correct, as most of my assumptions do. (I'm a bright fellow indeed, don't you think?) As I'm sure you have ascertained by now, I have amazing **(8)** (cognitive, cognative) skills.

Anyway, Vera was walking three dogs, whose **(9)** (heirarchy, hierarchy) was apparent as a German Shepard led the other two, which were a Boxer and a Pekinese. I could have wept when I saw Vera as she **(10)** (figuratively, literally) looked like a beautiful peacock adorned in radiant feathers of many colors. **(11)** (Figuratively, Literally), Vera was breathtakingly beautiful in a blue denim jacket, holey black jeans and a dirty Kansas City Royals baseball cap. Vera obviously possesses an **(12)** (inherant, inherent) **(13)** (aesthetic, asethetic) talent; in fact, come to think of it, one could say Vera is **(14)** (avant-garde, avente-guard) when it comes to fashion as I've seen a number of young girls imitate the way she dresses.

I jogged up from behind Vera and cooed, "Greetings, Vera, do you remember me?"

"Oh, you startled me! Well, of course I do—you're none other than the egotistical Casper Whipplesnade! I thought for a second that you might be Glenn Fengerpopper because you two look a lot a like."

I smiled, "Glenn must be a handsome person indeed, Vera."

Vera said, "Well, I wouldn't say that. Anyway, I'm surprised to see you again, Casper. How are you?"

"I'm just fine, Vera, my dear, and I certainly want you to know that I haven't forgotten you, not for a second. Why, I understand that you are now into **(15)** (athaletics, athletics) these days, including playing volleyball."

"How sweet of you to know this, Casper. I'm flattered, but what about the *chosen* ones you have pursued so earnestly this school year, Mr. Modesty? Though we don't attend the same school, I have heard of your rather hilarious romantic escapades during this school year."

I could feel my face turn red in embarrassment, a condition that seldom afflicts me. I stammered, "Vera, I'm shocked—yes, *shocked!* Wherever did you get the idea that I have pursued other girls the past few months?"

Oh, never mind, Casper, I can **(16)** (analyze, analize) your facial expression and know I'm right. Frankly, Casper, it is common knowledge that you have been dumped by a number of girls at your school, and everyone I know is laughing at you. But that's besides the point. What's the **(17)** (cataylist, catalyst) that caused you to look me up on such a frosty morn, or is this one of your weird "open" air type of **(18)** (labratory, laboratory) **(19)** (experments, experiments) you are conducting?"

"Well, Vera, to tell you the truth, after due consideration and taking into account the **(20)** (empirical, empiracal) evidence I observed regarding your **(21)** (benine, benign) and wholesome personality, I felt you actually were worthy of being a special friend of mind, even to the point of going on a date with me."

"What?" Vera screeched.

"Now, now, Vera, I know you probably feel unworthy of going on a date with me, the smart, handsome, and suave Casper Whipplesnade, but I assure you ..."

"Oh, Casper, you really are a scream, but I *assure* you that I have no interest in being a special friend of yours or going on a date with you. For one thing, you are much too conceited, and for another thing, I have been dating Farley Humperdither, a wonderful fellow student at the school we both attend, which is Prestige Private School, not Silliville Public **(22)** (Academy, Acadamy) where you attend."

"Vera, what has happened to you? You exhibit signs of a **(23)** (malignant, malignent) snobbery that will eventually cause you much grief! I would never have guessed you were such a snob! Why can't you be down-to-earth and humble like I am?" And with that parting shot, I spun around on my heel and headed for home, vowing—you guessed it—that I will <u>not</u> ask a girl for a date until I am at least 21 years old. Let me repeat that: I will <u>not</u> ask a girl for a date until I am at least 21 years old.

Yet, there is a girl by the name of Monica ... but no, I have finally learned my lesson. I will <u>not</u> subject myself to the possibility of eating even more humble pie. (You believe me, don't you?)

B *One of the following words in each set of four may be misspelled. Circle any misspelled word and spell it correctly in the space provided. Otherwise write "Correct" on the line.*

1. bibliography   atrophy   conotation   curriculum   _____

2. dormatory   genre   benign   analyze   _____

3. denotation   author   advisor   edema   _____

4. playiarism   etymology   calligraphy   edema   _____

5. empirical   diagnosis   caricature   democracy   _____

Carefully check your responses with those in the Answer Key.

Capital Letters

- Unlike common nouns, **proper nouns** are capitalized because they refer to **specific people, places, or things,** as these examples indicate:

common noun	proper noun
boy, girl, cousin	Bruce, Alisha, Morley
town, city, state	Clarinda, Omaha, Nebraska
street, avenue, highway	Elm Street, Fifth Avenue, Taconic Parkway
car, inn, college	Chevrolet, Fairfield Inn, Duke

- In addition, names of **specific** organizations, products, businesses, and religious groups should be capitalized:

Boy Scouts of America   Colgate toothpaste

Maxine's Salon   Methodists

- The pronoun **I** should be capitalized:

I will contact Karla to see if she knows when the bus leaves because **I** don't know and neither does Bob.

- The beginning of a **sentence** should be capitalized:

  Snow fell continuously for fifteen hours.

- The beginning of a **quotation** should be capitalized:

  "**M**om, do you think school will be called off tomorrow?" Billy asked.

  However, the first word of an interrupted quotation is *not* capitalized:

  "I do think school will be called off tomorrow, Billy," his mother replied, "**b**ut don't cry if it isn't."

- The first, last, and major words in a title should be capitalized; however, short words (*the, a, an, of, for*) within a title are generally not capitalized as you can see from studying the following examples:

  N is for Noose (book title)
  "**M**ack the **K**nife" (song title)
  "**L**earning the **B**asics of **W**atercoloring" (title of a magazine article)

  The exception to the above is if a short word begins the title, such as

  The Boys of Summer (book and movie title)
  "**F**or He's a Jolly Good Fellow" (song title)

- The title of a person should be capitalized when used with his or her name or when the title takes the place of the person's name:

  The prayer was offered by **C**haplain **B**ezanson.
  Thank you, **C**haplain, for offering the prayer.

Don't, however, capitalize the title when used in a general way:

Chaplain Kendrick is from Illinois

vs.

The chaplain is from Illinois.

Aunt <u>M</u>indy will be retiring this spring.

vs.

My <u>a</u>unt will be retiring this spring.

<u>D</u>r. Jackson's office is in the <u>S</u>heffield <u>B</u>uilding.

vs.

The <u>d</u>octor's office is in this <u>b</u>uilding.

EXERCISE 10.1 *On the line provided, rewrite words in the following sentences that contain a capitalization error. If no error is present, write "correct" on the line.*

1. my son loves cheerios for breakfast and wheaties after school.

_____

2. Dr. Balston has been our Doctor for many years.

_____

3. "We now live in Tennessee," my in-laws said, "And we love it."

_____

4. " i don't belong to kiwanis, but my brother Wilbur does."

_____

5. The Catholic church in our Community is remodeling its educational wing.

_____

6. My five-year-old Nephew sings "Jingle bells" all year long.

_____

7. We rented a car from Hertz and drove much of the day on the pennsylvania Turnpike.

_____

8. Do you think the Eagle's Nest would be a good Restaurant to take our Friends this Weekend?

_____

9. one of my favorite Teachers is Professor Khu.

_____

10. Ted's son is a forward on the Lenox Tigers Basketball team.

_____

11. Whenever my Aunts and Uncles get together, they end up having an argument about Politics.

_____

12. Brandon, be careful driving on Maxwell Street because of its many frost heaves and potholes.

_____

SET B

- Names of holidays, months, and days of the week are capitalized, but <u>NOT</u> seasons of the year (spring, summer, fall, winter):

  What do you want for **C**hristmas?
  Maxine's birthday is in **S**eptember.
  Do you work **M**ondays through **F**ridays?

- Names of languages and nationalities should be capitalized:

  French, **S**panish, **M**andarin
  Italian, **S**wiss, **G**erman

- Historical documents and events as well as specific regions should be capitalized:

  Declaration of **I**ndependence
  Boston **T**ea **P**arty
  Atlanta is in the **S**outh, and **D**enver is in the **W**est.

  Note: Compass directions are **NOT** capitalized:

  We drove **<u>south</u>** on Highway 71.
  The business section is a few miles **<u>north</u>** of this intersection.
  There's a big lake seven miles to the **<u>east</u>** of Sioux City, Iowa.
  Nebraska is **<u>west</u>** of Iowa.

- Names of school subjects should be capitalized **IF** they are names of languages (**E**nglish, **S**panish, et. al.), or **IF** they have special numbers or letters after them:

  Political Science 300   Biology 100A

EXERCISE 10.2 *On the line provided, rewrite any words in the following sentences that contain a capitalization error. If the sentence contains no errors, write "correct" on the line.*

1. Lincoln delivered the *gettysburg address* in november, 1863.

_____

2. Paul is of French ancestry.

_____

3. sunday is the first day of Spring.

_____

4. I took economics last semester, and I'm taking a business course this semester.

_____

5. The San Francisco Bay area is beautiful, especially in the Spring and Fall.

_____

6. My closest neighbors are retired, and they spend January through March in arizona.

_____

7. I think spanish is a beautiful sounding Language.

_____

8. The louisiana purchase occurred in 1803.

_____

9. Harriet switched her major from french to Biology.

_____

10. On March 13, 1988, our oldest granddaughter was born.

_____

✔ CHECK-UP: Chapter 10, Capital Letters

Circle the words in the following sentences that should or should not begin with a capital letter. Then write the word as it should be spelled on the line provided. If a sentence is correct as it is, write **correct** *on the line.*

1. The song "My girl" was one of the Temptations' biggest hits.

_____

2. How was the Weather when you were in vermont this past Winter, Pastor Logan?

_____

3. Bruiser works at Peg of My Heart, an irish pub, on Tuesdays, Thursdays, and Saturdays.

_____

4. Juanita inquired, "when will Gus get back from egypt?

_____

5. "Actually, the first and last movie I ever saw," Wendell said, "was *lassie come home* at the rialto theater in Provo, utah, during the Summer of 1946."

_____

6. Jamie gushed, "i know you're old, wendall, but are you really that old?"

_____

7. The original copy of the *Emancipation Proclamation* is kept at the National Archives in Washington, D. C.

_____

POST-ASSESSMENT BEGINS ON THE NEXT PAGE

POST-ASSESSMENT

Chapter 1: Noun Plurals

Write the plural form of the following words.

singular	*plural*
1. picture	_____
2. echo	_____
3. attorney-at-law	_____
4. Kennedy	_____
5. maid of honor	_____
6. life	_____
7. psychosis	_____
8. fish	_____
9. pony	_____
10. potato	_____

Chapter 2: -ie and -ei Words

Neatly circle the correctly spelled word.

1. sceince   science
2. achieve   acheive
3. cieling   ceiling
4. yeild   yield
5. anceint   ancient

6. belief   beleif
7. receipt   reciept
8. their   thier
9. vein   vien
10. foriegn   foreign

Chapter 3: Vowel Suffixes

On the line provided, spell each word after adding the vowel suffix __-ed__.

1. submit _____
2. regret _____
3. explain _____
4. prefer _____
5. order _____

6. enter _____
7. control _____
8. beg _____
9. quiz _____
10. burn _____

Chapter 1: Prefixes, Compounds, Consonant Suffixes, Final -y Words

On the line provided, spell each word after adding the indicate prefix, compound, or consonant suffix.

1. dis + satisfied _____

2. un + natural _____

3. mis + spell _____

4. in + numerable _____

5. un + necessary _____

6. team + mate _____

7. manage + ment _____

8. book + keeper _____

9. ear + rings _____

10. care + ful _____

11. time + ly _____

12. lone + ly _____

13. easy + ly _____

14. room + mate _____

15. tail + light _____

16. hurry + ing _____

17. ugly   +   ness   _____

18. angry   +   ly   _____

19. dis   +   similar   _____

20. dare   +   devil   _____

Chapters 5 and 6: Words Frequently Confused

After studying the sentence, circle the appropriate word in parentheses; then write this word on the line provided.

_____ 1. Snowball, our cat, clawed a (hole, whole) in our sofa, (than, then) he slept the (hole, whole) day on my recliner.

_____ 2. Is it better to rent or to buy a car, Casper? What's your (advice, advise)? Grampa will probably (advice, advise) me to buy a horse, I'm sure.

_____ 3. (There, Their, They're) home is just (passed, past) Phillips Park on the left side of the road.

_____ 4. Do you think this miserable (weather, whether) will (affect, effect) (their, there, they're) traveling plans?

_____ 5. Would you prefer macaroni and cheese rather (than, then) the spaghetti and meatballs special, Bubba?

_____ 6. Does Lois Lane's decision (to, too, two) leave her job at *The Daily Planet* have any (affect, effect) on your future plans, Clark Kent?

_____ 7 How in the world did all those shingles become (loose, lose), Reggie?

_____ 8. Monsieur, may I read the letter you received from Madame Bovary, or is it (to, too, two) (personal, personnel)?

_____ 9. In the (passed, past), our family used to go to Aunt Edie's for Thanksgiving, but now she comes to our home for this holiday.

_____ 10. Mr. Werewolf, do you think the moon will ever (shine, shown) again this month?

Chapters 7 and 8: Spelling Challenges

A *On the line provided, correctly spell the word suggested in parentheses.*

_____ 1. Did you (suceed, succeed) in getting the mortgage to buy the house, Jesse?

_____ 2. Did a bank official give you a (definite, defanite) answer?

_____ 3. Are you (familiar, familar) with Mr. Scrooge, the bank president, Jesse?

_____ 4. I'm confident Mr. Jiminy Cricket would (reccomend, recommend) me for a chirping position in the Bitty Bird Band.

_____ 5. Was Groucho a (discipline, dissipline) problem when he went to school?

_____ 6. Amanda is studying to be a (docter, doctor) at Ohio State University.

_____ 7. The weather was finally (pleasent, pleasant), so Karla and I went on a long bicycle ride throughout the city.

_____ 8. Do you think our landlord has a (predjudice, prejudice) against all pets, including rhinos and canaries?

_____ 9. Gloria, did I (embarrass, embarass) you in front of your boyfriend by asking him how much money he makes as a counterfeiter?

_____ 10. My roommate has to improve his grades if he wants to stay (eligible, elegible) for the chess team.

B *Write the correctly spelled word on the line provided.*

_____ 1. tomorrow, tommorow

_____ 2. amateur, amatuer

_____ 3. parallel, paralell

_____ 4. gaurentee, guarantee

_____ 5. vaccum, vacuum

_____ 6. comittee, committee

_____ 7. exercise, exerise

_____ 8. neccessary, necessary

_____ 9. license, lisence

_____ 10. Wensday, Wednesday

Chapter 9: Academic Words

Complete the spelling of each academic word suggested. The space mark or marks in each word (-) indicate that one or more letters are missing.

1. ac-d-mic _____

2. col-ge _____

3. sop-more _____

4. lit-rat-re _____

5. envir-ment _____

6. lab-rat-ry _____

7. for-gn _____

8. hyp-th-s _____

9. math-matics _____

10. ath-tics _____

Chapter 10: Capital Letters

Circle the letters in words that <u>should</u> or <u>should not</u> be capitalized; then correctly rewrite these words on the line provided. If all the words in a sentence are capitalized correctly, then write "correct" on the line.

1. Vivian studied spanish for two years in High School.

   _____

2. Billy Bob, who lives in Bennington, Vermont, got a flat tire while driving near the shore of lake Champlain.

   _____

3. My brother Leon once owned a red ryder beebee gun that he received on his 14th birthday; he's now 56, and he still treasures this gun.

   _____

4. Dad's all-time favorite movie is *Singin' in the Rain* and Mom's is *A History of Violence.* Go figure.

   _____

5. Mark says that spurgeon's furniture store would be a good place to buy a new sofa.

   _____

6. The Iowa Capitol Building is an impressive structure both inside and out.

   _____

7. Cappy served in the u.s. navy on an Aircraft Carrier for over twenty years.

   _____

8. *Double Trouble* was one of my favorite books when i was growing up.

   _____

9. "What do you mean," Freeda interjected, "By saying I'm sometimes rude and hard to get along with, you Creep?"

_____

10. "When I was a youngster living in the midwest," Bean Ball said, "I wanted to be a rootin' tootin' cowboy," Bean Ball continued, "But now that I'm living in a Jungle, I have my heart set on being a fearless Lion Tamer."

_____

The Answer Key for Sentence Matters follows. Be conscientious in checking your answers on the exercises, assessments, and Check-Ups as it's easy to unintentionally make an error.

ANSWER KEY

PRE-ASSESSMENT

Chapter 1, Noun Plurals

1. donkeys
2. valleys
3. communities
4. apologies
5. solos
6. halves
7. mothers-in-law
8. canoes
9. buses
10. churches

Chapter 2, *-ei, -ie* words

1. thief
2. weight
3. believe
4. niece
5. ceiling
6. field
7. vein
8. neighbor
9. seizure
10. belief

Chapter 3, Vowel Suffixes []

1. jogging
2. occurred
3. swimming
4. quizzing
5. preferred
6. courageous
7. picnicked
8. changeable
9. famous
10. inconceivable

Chapter 4, Prefixes, Consonant Suffixes, Final -y Words

1. background
2. roommate
3. Murphys
4. management
5. glorious
6. studies
7. bookkeeper
8. happiness
9. unnecessary
10. mailbox

Chapter 5 and 6: Words Frequently Confused

1. passed, effect
2. past
3. than
4. advice, wear
5. their, whole, there
6. They're, too, there
7. Where
8. quite, it's
9. course
10. plain
11. personnel
12. through
13. lose
14. capital
15. except
16. conscious, too, personal, conscience

Chapters 7 and 8: Spelling Challenges

1. incidentally
2. acquittal
3. *correct*
4. *correct*
5. amateur
6. miniature
7. *correct*
8. *correct*
9. recommend
10. environment
11. boundary
12. sophomore
13. *correct*
14. mathematics
15. quantity
16. occurrence
17. discipline
18. committee
19. accommodate
20. advisable

Chapter 9: Academic Words

1. hypothesis
2. behavior
3. cognitive
4. catalyst
5. analyze
6. benign
7. malignant
8. empirical
9. curriculum
10. author

Chapter 10: Capital Words

1. *correct*
2. Have
3. cowboys
4. but
5. *correct*
6. national holiday, United States of America
7. uncle, aunt, Minnesota, Florida
8. Snoopy, *War and Peace*, century
9. science, geography, algebra, sophomore
10. Canada, Quebec City, Canada

ANSWER KEY FOR THE CHAPTER EXERCISES

Chapter 1: Noun Plurals

Exercise 1.1 (p. 1)

1. trees
2. animals
3. chairs
4. magazines
5. basketballs

Exercise 1.2 (p. 2)

1. daughter-in-law
2. commanders-in-chief
3. runners-up
4. drive-ins
5. mothers-in-law

Exercise 1.3 (p. 3)

1. beaches
2. glasses
3. waltzes
4. crashes
5. foxes

Exercise 1.4 (p. 4)

1. McKays
2. armies
3. Fridays
4. countries
5. Kennedys
6. subways

Exercise 1.5 (p. 6)

1. vetoes
2. patios
3. tornadoes *or* tornados
4. solos
5. radios
6. embargoes
7. mosquitoes *or* mosquitos
8. videos
9. buffaloes, buffalos *or just* buffalo
10. potatoes

Exercise 1.6 (p. 8)

1. loaves
2. chiefs
3. scarfs *or* scarves
4. elves
5. proofs
6. thieves
7. lives
8. reefs
9. tariffs
10. gulfs

Exercise 1.7 (p. 9)

1. teeth
2. mice
3. parentheses
4. sheep
5. crises
6. oases
7. oxen
8. women
9. diagnoses
10. salmon

Check-Up, Chapter 1

(p. 10)

A

1. potatoes	6. boxes	11. beliefs	16. analyses
2. pianos	7. women	12. yourselves	17. theses
3. heroes	8. thieves	13. crises	18. latches
4. echoes	9. sheriffs	14. fish	19. maids of honor
5. sons-in-law	10. wives	15. sheep	20. bushes

(p. 11)

B

1. cliffs	6. tomatoes	11. churches	16. hawks
2. pastries	7. echoes	12. moose	17. families
3. donkeys	8. lunches	13. attorneys-at-law	18. prescriptions
4. batteries	9. Kennedys	14. mice	19. matches
5. themselves	10. valleys	15. children	20. analyses

(p. 12)

C

1. True	3. True	5. False	7. False	9. False
2. False	4. False	6. True	8. True	10. False

Chapter 2: *-ei* and *-ie* Words

Exercise 2.1 (p. 14)

1. friends
2. niece, grief
3. friend, chief, shriek
4. field, cashier, priest
5. believe, fierce, quiet, boyfriend
6. relief, believe
7. shield, yield, achieve, quiet

Exercise 2.2 (p. 16)

1. hygiene
2. obedient
3. field
4. shield
5. wield
6. shriek
7. height

Exercise 2.3 (p. 17)

1. *correct*	7. *correct*	13. *correct*
2. veins	8. deceive	14. *correct*
3. ceiling	9. *correct*	15. *correct*
4. feign	10. reign	16. weight
5. *correct*	11. *correct*	17. veil
6. neighbor	12. heinous	

Exercise 2.4 (p. 19)

1. forfeit	5. foreign	8. Fahrenheit	11. heir, financier
2. protein	6. ancient	9. weird, neighbor	12. heifer, shriek
3. proficient	7. science	10. leisure, efficient	13. conscience, sufficient
4. Neither			

Check-Up, Chapter 2

(p. 21)

A
1. neighbor
2. yield
3. cashier
4. brief
5. ceiling
6. shriek
7. weigh
8. deceive
9. believe
10. receive
11. freight

(p. 22)

B
1. niece
2. chief
3. heinous
4. reign
5. conceit
6. heir
7. science
8. financier

Chapter 3: Vowel Suffixes

Exercise 3.1 (p. 25)

1. digging
2. occurred
3. brighter
4. quizzed
5. jogged
6. wrapping
7. transferred
8. bigger
9. dropped
10. jumping
11. begged
12. admitting
13. slammed
14. quitting
15. swimming

Exercise 3.2 (p. 27)

1. inferred
2. inferring
3. inference
4. noticed
5. noticing
6. noticeable
7. indulged
8. indulging
9. indulgence
10. preferred
11. preferring
12. preference
13. having
14. writing
15. picnicked
16. picnicking
17. peaceable
18. desirable
19. caring
20. panicking

Check-Up, Chapter 3

A Ginger (p. 29)

1. outrageous
2. courageous
3. noticeable
4. writing
5. inferred
6. ignoring
7. frolicking
8. preferred
9. committed
10. proceeded
11. interrupting
12. hoping
13. panicky
14. desirable
15. escaping
16. sincerity
17. reference
18. dating
19. discovered
20. humiliated

B (p. 31)

1. writing
2. smoking
3. bleeding
4. conference
5. inconceivable
6. wagging
7. gulped
8. fibbing
9. junking
10. grazing
11. quizzed
12. popped
13. preference
14. preferred
15. panicked
16. mimicking
17. changeable
18. blazing
19. aspirations
20. ranging

Chapter 4: Prefixes, Compounds. Consonant Suffixes, Final -*y* Words

Exercise 4.1 (p. 34)

1. unnatural
2. dissatisfied
3. windshield
4. earrings
5. misspelled
6. keyboard
7. salesclerk
8. reexamined
9. subsoil
10. backbone

Exercise 4.2 (p. 37)

1. parties
2. wristwatch
3. actually
4. confinement
5. peacefully
6. announcement
7. happiness
8. delightfully
9. misspell
10. silverware

Check-Up, Chapter 4: Deep Death Canyon (p. 37)

1. absolutely
2. hesitantly
3. practically
4. mercifully
5. finally
6. glorious
7. firsthand
8. lifetime
9. amusement
10. backpack
11. tragedies
12. fantasies
13. courageous
14. eventually
15. traveling
16. endless
17. countries
18. accusingly
19. buddies
20. Actually
21. putting
22. wearily
23. enemies
24. crudeness
25. upbeat
26. pancakes
27. ceaseless
28. powerless
29. relentless
30. sunscreen
31. already
32. painfully
33. without
34. barefoot
35. footprint
36. dizziness
37. panickly
38. rattlesnake
39. grasshoppers
40. lazily
41. themselves
42. nearby
43. sunburned
44. backbone
45. highway
46. restaurant
47. overpass
48. ourselves
49. restroom
50. apiece
51. relating
52. humankind
53. parties
54. unlikely

Chapter 5: Words Frequently Confused — 1

Exercise 5.1 (p. 45)

1. breathe, breath, an
2. a, effect, affect
3. capital, capitol
4. accept, a, an
5. brakes, break
6. cloths, clothes
7. advise, advice

Exercise 5.3 (p. 50)

1. eminent, imminent
2. loose
3. Desert
4. further
5. It's, whole
6. device, devised
7. forth
8. its
9. fourth
10. dessert
11. hole
12. desert
13. brake

Answers to Exercises 5.2 and 5.4 will vary.

Check-Up, Chapter 5 (p. 54)

1. advice
2. fourth
3. capital, an
4. devise
5. imminent
6. whole, desert
7. clothes, it's
8. loose
9. except
10. break, lose, breath
11. advise
12. dessert
13. brake
14. accept
15. breathe
16. capitol
17. cloths
18. A, a, device, it's, its
19. affect, effect
20. eminent, forth
21. farther, further
22. hole

Chapter 6: Words Frequently Confused — 2

Exercise 6.1 (p. 59)

1. through, two, then, threw, to, to, too
2. there, their, they're, there
3. quiet, quit, quite
4. principal, principle
5. shone, shown
6. then, than
7. plain, plane, plain

Exercise 6.3 (p. 65)

1. Whether, weather
2. past, passed
3. course
4. where
5. conscience
6. You're
7. conscious
8. complement
9. your, your, personal
10. wear
11. course, coarse
12. compliment, personnel, your

Answers to Exercise 6.2 will vary.

Check-Up, Chapter 6 (p. 67)

1. then
2. your, complement, your, compliment, your
3. threw, through
4. weather, too, two, to
5. Whether, wear, where
6. quiet, where, quit, quite
7. their, there, your, They're, quite, quite
8. you're, your, than, too, personal
9. conscious, personnel, passed, past, conscience, wearing, its, coarse
10. conscious, plane, It's, plain, your
11. shown, shone

Chapter 7: Spelling Challenges — 1

Exercise 7.1 (p. 71)

1. accidentally
2. *correct*
3. valuable
4. acquire
5. arctic
6. boundary
7. *correct*
8. *correct*
9. parliament
10. coincidentally
11. tragedy
12. acquaint
13. miniature
14. practically
15. basically
16. quandary
17. *correct*
18. *correct*
19. probably
20. liable
21. acquittal

Exercise 7.2 (p. 74)

1. mathematics
2. recognize
3. environment
4. bachelor
5. recommend
6. grandmother
7. chocolate
8. *correct*
9. candidate
10. *correct*
11. exercise
12. sophomore
13. *correct*
14. discipline
15. grandfather
16. *correct*
17. *correct*
18. *correct*
19. congratulate
20. punctuation

Exercise 7.3 (p. 78)

1. restaurant
2. definite
3. guarantee
4. among
5. *correct*
6. rhythm
7. *correct*
8. absence
9. tomorrow
10. *correct*
11. *correct*
12. separate
13. *correct*
14. *correct*
15. privilege
16. *correct*
17. explanation
18. *correct*
19. embarrass
20. *correct*

Check-Up, Chapter 7

A Veronica Pringleagogo (p. 79)

1. definitely
2. occasions
3. candidate
4. privilege
5. acquainted
6. cousin
7. among
8. parallel
9. valuable
10. liable
11. accidentally
12. congratulate
13. separate
14. calendar
15. restaurant
16. chocolate
17. exercise
18. miniature
19. embarrassed
20. practically
21. discipline
22. succeed
23. amateurs
24. accommodate
25. rhythm
26. among
27. acquired
28. Incidentally
29. probably
30. recognized
31. temperament
32. occurrence
33. absence

B (p. 83)

1. parallel
2. license
3. eligible
4. explanation
5. guarantee
6. vacuum
7. committee
8. Tomorrow, grandfather, grandmother
9. sandwich
10. familiar
11. bachelor
12. sophomore, mathematics
13. punctuation
14. dilemma, quandary
15. boundary
16. Parliament
17. business
18. occurrence
19. criticism, environment
20. quantity
21. dialect
22. probably
23. acquire
24. Coincidentally
25. acquittal
26. arctic
27. basically, exercise
28. recommended
29. accommodate
30. rhythm

Chapter 8: Spelling Challenges — 2

Exercise 8.1 (p. 88)

1. Caribbean
2. drunkenness
3. *correct*
4. February
5. *correct*
6. college
7. apparent
8. foreign
9. category
10. *correct*
11. difference
12. gauge
13. *correct*
14. *correct*
15. friend
16. argument
17. *correct*
18. believe
19. collectible
20. *correct*

Exercise 8.2 (p. 91)

1. *correct*
2. independent
3. *correct*
4. leisure
5. poison
6. *correct*
7. intelligence
8. noticeable
9. height
10. maintenance
11. guidance
12. *correct*
13. *correct*
14. *correct*
15. jewelry
16. *correct*
17. ignorance
18. *correct*
19. liaison
20. mischievous

Exercise 8.3 (p. 94)

1. fascinate
2. hunger
3. ghastly
4. monstrous
5. questionnaire
6. scissors
7. plumber
8. ninth
9. entrance
10. adolescent
11. remembrance
12. judgment
13. argument
14. knowledge
15. acknowledgement
16. truly
17. subtle
18. disastrous
19. benign
20. prompt
21. column
22. mnemonics
23. straight
24. Wednesday
25. solemn
26. hindrance

Check-Up, Chapter 8

A (p. 96) **Edith Esterhelmsly**

1. ghastly
2. disastrous
3. pronunciation
4. intelligence
5. apparent
6. believed
7. guidance
8. truly
9. difference
10. heights
11. hindrance
12. fascinating
13. adolescent
14. subtle
15. mischievous
16. argument
17. original
18. collectible
19. judgment
20. athletic
21. hygiene
22. ignorance
23. knowledge
24. achieved
25. maintenance
26. column
27. straight
28. noticeable
29. canceled
30. solemn
31. poison
32. entrance
33. changeable
34. leisure
35. college
36. remembrance
37. neighbors

B (p. 100)

1. achieve
2. Caribbean, drunkenness
3. *correct*
4. *correct*
5. mediocre, liaison, dumbbell
6. advisable
7. collectible, February

Chapter 9: Academic Words

Exercise 9.1 (p. 105)

1. environment
2. inductive
3. author
4. catalyst
5. adviser/advisor
6. hyperbole
7. calligraphy
8. behavior
9. avant-garde
10. curriculum
11. premise
12. caricature
13. apparatus
14. deduction
15. athletics
16. experiment
17. aesthetic
18. academy
19. democracy
20. dormant
21. dormitory
22. diagnosis
23. commencement

Exercise 9.2 (p. 110)

1. laboratory
2. inherent
3. connotation
4. denotation
5. hierarchy
6. plagiarism
7. bibliography
8. Carpe diem
9. etymology
10. analyze
11. hypothesis
12. empirical
13. atrophy
14. edema
15. cognitive
16. genre
17. literal
18. figurative
19. malignant
20. benign

Check-Up, Chapter 9

A Vera Venuslike (p. 112)

1. deduction
2. environment
3. dormant
4. hypothesis
5. behavior
6. commencement
7. carpe diem
8. cognitive
9. hierarchy
10. figuratively
11. Literally
12. inherent
13. aesthetic
14. avant-garde
15. athletics
16. analyze
17. catalyst
18. laboratory
19. experiments
20. empirical
21. benign
22. Academy
23. malignant

B (p. 115)

1. connotation
2. dormitory
3. *correct*
4. plagiarism
5. *correct*

Chapter 10: Capital Letters

Exercise 10.1 (p. 118)

1. My, Cheerios, Wheaties
2. doctor
3. and
4. I, Kiwanis
5. community
6. nephew, Bells
7. Pennsylvania
8. restaurant, friends, weekend
9. One, teachers
10. basketball
11. aunts, uncles, politics
12. *correct*

Exercise 10.2 (p. 121)

1. *Gettysburg Address,* November
2. *correct*
3. Sunday, spring
4. *correct*
5. spring, fall
6. Arizona
7. Spanish, language
8. Louisiana Purchase
9. French, biology
10. correct

Check-Up, Chapter 10 (p. 122)

1. Girl
2. weather, Vermont, winter
3. Irish
4. When, Egypt
5. *Lassie Come Home,* Rialto Theater, Utah, summer
6. I, Wendall
7. *correct*

POST-ASSESSMENT ANSWER KEY

Chapter 1: Noun Plurals

1. pictures
2. echoes
3. attorneys-at-law
4. Kennedys
5. maids of honor
6. lives
7. psychoses
8. fish
9. ponies
10. potatoes

Chapter 2: *-ie* and *-ei* Words

1. science
2. achieve
3. ceiling
4. yield
5. ancient
6. belief
7. receipt
8. their
9. vein
10. foreign

Chapter 3: Vowel Suffixes

1. submitted
2. regretted
3. explained
4. preferred
5. ordered
6. entered
7. controlled
8. begged
9. quizzed
10. burned

Chapter 4: Prefixes, Compounds, Consonant Suffixes, Final *-y* Words

1. dissatisfied
2. unnatural
3. misspell
4. innumerable
5. unnecessary
6. teammate
7. management
8. bookkeeper
9. earrings
10. careful
11. timely
12. lonely
13. easily
14. roommate
15. taillight
16. hurrying
17. ugliness
18. angrily
19. dissimilar
20. daredevil

Chapter 5 & 6. Words Frequently Confused

1. hole, then, whole
2. advice, advise
3. Their, past
4. weather, affect, their
5. than
6. to, effect
7. loose
8. too, personal
9. past
10. shine

Chapters 7 and 8: Spelling Challenges

A	B
1. succeed	1. tomorrow
2. definite	2. amateur
3. familiar	3. parallel
4. recommend	4. guarantee
5. discipline	5. vacuum
6. doctor	6. committee
7. pleasant	7. exercise
8. prejudice	8. necessary
9. embarrass	9. license
10. eligible	10. Wednesday

Chapter 9: Academic Words

1. academic
2. college
3. sophomore
4. literature
5. environment
6. laboratory
7. foreign
8. hypothesis
9. mathematics
10. athletics

Chapter 10: Capital Letters

1. <u>S</u>panish, high school
2. <u>L</u>ake
3. <u>R</u>ed <u>R</u>yder
4. *Correct*
5. <u>S</u>purgeon's <u>F</u>urniture <u>S</u>tore
6. *Correct*
7. <u>U.S.</u> Navy, aircraft carrier
8. <u>I</u>
9. by, creep
10. <u>M</u>idwest, but, jungle, lion tamer

ABOUT THE AUTHOR

R. Kent Smith, EdD, is an experienced instructor of literary skills, having taught from the elementary through college levels, culminating in twenty-nine years as professor of developmental studies at the University of Maine. He has authored several textbooks, including eight editions of *Building Vocabulary for College*.

Shawn J. Smith, PhD, has been a learning specialist at public and private high schools in the Boston area for twenty-five years and also enjoys a thriving private tutoring practice.

INDEX

picnicked, picnicking 27

piece 14

pierce 14

plagiarism 110

plain *vs.* plane 57

plumber 93

plurals

    compound words 2

    irregular nouns 8

    proper names ending in *-y* 4

    words ending in *-is* 9

    words that end in *-f* and *-fe* 7

    words that end in *-o* 6

poison 90

pony

    pl. ponies 3

potato

    pl. potatoes 5

practically 71

prefer 23, 26

    preference 26

    preferred, preferring 23

premise 104

priest 14

principal *vs.* principle 57

privilege 77

probably 70

proficient 19

prompt 93

pronunciation 91

punctuation 73

Q

quandary 70

quantity 74

questionnaire 93

quiet 14

quip

    quipped, quipping 24

quit

quitting 24

quit, quiet, quite 58

quiz

    quizzed, quizzing 24

R

radio

    pl. radios 4

receipt 16

receive 16

recognize 74

recommend 74

reef

    pl. reefs 7

refer

    reference 26

reign 16

relief 14

remember

    remembrance 93

restaurant 77

retrieve 14

rhythm 77

S

salmon

    pl. salmon 9

sandwich 73

scarf

    pl. scarfs or scarves 7

science 19

scissors 93

separate 77

sheep

    pl. sheep 9

sheriff

    pl. sheriffs 7

shield 14

shone *vs.* shown 58

shriek 14

siege 14

sincere

    sincerity 26

sleigh 16

solemn 93

solo

    pl. solos 5

son-in-law

    pl. sons-in-law 2

sophomore 74

soprano

    pl. sopranos 5

sovereign 19

straight 93

studio

    pl. studios 4

subtle 93

surveillance 16

T

tariff

    pl. tariffs 7

temperament 70

than *vs.* then 58

their, there, they're 58

threw *vs.* through 58

tomato

    pl. tomatoes 5

tomorrow 77

tooth

    pl. teeth 8

tornado

    pl. tornados or tornadoes 6

to, too, two 59

tragedy 71

transfer 24, 25

    transferring, transferred 24

trout

    pl. trout 9

true

    truly 94

V

vacuum 77

valuable 70

veil 16

vein 16

volcano

    pl. volcanos or volcanoes 6

W

wear *vs.* where 64

weather *vs.* whether 64

Wednesday 93

weigh 16

weird 19

wharf

    pl. wharfs or wharves 7

wield 14

wolf

    pl. wolves 7

woman

    pl. women 8

write

    writing 26

Y

yield 14

your *vs.* you're 64

Z

zoo

    pl. zoos 4

Printed in the United States
By Bookmasters